Marriage WORK BOOK

*Enjoying and Making Your Marriage
Work Out and Last Long*

SEYI OLADOSU

Marriage Workbook

Published in the United Kingdom by Seyi Oladosu Publishing

ISBN: 978-1-7392146-2-3

DEDICATION

This book is dedicated to all married couples sacrificing to make their marriage better, healthier, stronger, sweeter, sensational, affectionate, more intimate, more enriched and built to last. Keep on staying strong and stronger. Keep the flame alive. Heaven on Earth is real and assured.

CONTENTS

ACKNOWLEDGEMENT

This book wouldn't have been possible if not for God almighty. I give Him all the glory for the grace to have practical experiences and insights to journal and for how far He has helped all the way during favourable and unfavorable times to understand the possibilities of heaven on earth in a marital destiny. Thanks Lord for fruitfulness, life, family, guidance, progress, counsels, teachings, instructions and leadership for our marital structure. Thank you Lord for peace, love, joy, turn arounds, compatibility, adaptations, submissions, kindnesses, mercy, goodness of God. Bless the Lord oh my soul and all that's within me bless His holy name.

Thanks Lord for victories over battles of life, for troubles, pains, for celebrations, successes, failures, testimonies; for many are the afflictions of the righteous, but the Lord delivers them out of them all.

Glory be to God. For we know that all things work together for the good of them that love the Lord and who are called according to His purpose.

I really appreciate Kemi, my lovely wife, for doing life together through our ups and downs. We've grown in all beautiful, excellent, exceptional dimensions even through adversities over the years. Praise God for silencing the adversaries. Thanks for making life good, your affection, considerations, care, love and kindness is a difference maker.

To Ayooluwa and Ibukunoluwa, we appreciate God for you. It's been amazing parenting and pastoring you, your golden touches, wisdom, considerations, thoughtfulness, philosophical depths, caring hearts, brilliance, beautiful minds, zeal and love for God strengthened and made us better and more agile.

Our seasoned parents, Bishop I F & Lady E A Oladosu; Sir S K & Lady J B Osinoiki; led the way, laid a solid family and marital foundation worthy of emulation and big follow, so grateful for your life of big sacrifice, enduring faith, integrity, faithfulness. Thank you for your exemplary life. Two families that came together in 1993, gave rise to the third family and became three in one. We are blessed beyond measure.

What more can be said of our Spiritual leaders, Pastors, Mentors, fathers, mothers. Daddy & Mummy G O; Pastor J F Odesola & Mummy Bisi Racheal, Rev George, Dr Charles Stanley (of blessed memory). A lot was learnt through your practical living, counseling, prayers, good environments to create laudable unforgettable memories, teachings, sit downs, close & afar of mentoring. Your timely words of wisdom can't be overemphasized.

I'm so much indebted and grateful to my great friend and a most unique destiny helper, Pastor Fatai Kasali for arranging, supervising, organising and making sure this book was released on time with excellence and professional touch. Thanks to God for your heart of gold.

So glad for all my associates who had one input or the other as we all journey through life, journey of a lifetime; Pastors Segun Adenuga, Femi David, James Adeyemi, Dare Orelusi, Felix Makanjuola jnr, Made Okunromade, Florence Enughuren, Godday Okosun.

Thanks to all my distinguished friends, brothers and sisters from another mother, Wole Fatiregun, Dr Dayo & Ola Adeyemo, Dr Fola & Toyin Adekusibe, Dr Charles & Yinka Omole, Prof Edwin & Dr Hephzibah Egede, Dr Gbeminiyi Eboda, Kayode & Kela Oladapo, Pastors Kunle & Simi Olushola, Pastors Babatunde & Abi Ogunsola. Awesome times of fellowship, bonding, association, collaborations, comradeship and partnership.

PREFACE

You can have Heaven on Earth in your marriage. Anytime I say this to people, many look at me like I've lost my mind and don't know what I'm talking about.

But the truth actually is that with God's help and goodness, your marriage can be a beautiful reference point.

Marriages these days don't seem to last as long as desired. Intending couples are so focused on the wedding day that it didn't occur to them to plan for the future—the long haul. I still can't get out of my mind a couple who wanted the wedding vow to read: "FOR RICHER FOR RICHER, FOR HEALTH FOR HEALTHY, FOR BETTER FOR BETTER".

So, what happens in the days of lack, sickness, or when things get worse in the course of marriage? The question is, will you run away?

This book provides answers to bugging issues of life and difficult situations as applicable to spouse management, time management, and money management. It will also address communication breakdowns, loss of affection, health issues, or simply people just growing apart. In fact, 65% of marriages that end in divorce are because of money problems.

A lot of marriages have no reason to crash if certain things are put into place. We should have consideration for one another, putting God first, seeking God's face, and adapting to systems that can promote peace, love, joy, wellness, vitality, and prosperity.

You can't change people around you, but you can change how you let them affect you and how you also affect them in all beautiful, cool running, considerable ways. Learning to sacrifice for your loved ones provides an open door and creates greater room to maximise your relationship and get the best out of it.

Your spouse is God's best gift for you to fulfil destiny and live a purpose-driven life. I pray you shall be jointly and rightly fitted together as in a square peg in a square hole with the bone of your bone and the flesh of your flesh.

Learning about your spouse enables you to know them very well and have a good balance to understand, relate to, and enjoy the best from them. Marriage is supposed to make us better and not bitter. It is meant to be enjoyed and not endured. To complement and not to compete.

Many people who are married want to give up, while some want to remarry.

Some people desire to get married for the first time ever. As long as we don't throw in the towel, there is always a way out of any jam or predicament.

There's hope for a tree that, even at the scent of water, it can spring forth again and bud to bear fruit.

Welcome to Marriage Workbook! Welcome to an endless love journey and affectionate discoveries.

Welcome to possibilities.

Welcome to reality.

Welcome to dreams and visions.

Welcome to real-life experience.

Welcome to growing up and maturity.

Lots and lots of work in progress.

Welcome to the glorious future.

If you work at it, it will work out very well. There's a lot of room for improvement. The best is yet to come.

Chapter One

STRENGTHENING YOUR CONNECTION

Marriage is God-ordained and designed to be the closest possible relationship, characterised by increasing intimacy and growing interdependence. However, this is not automatic. We must continue to work on our marriage if we're to stay closely connected.

Marriage can be compared to tending or cultivating a vineyard.

FOUR ANALOGIES FOR TENDING A MARRIAGE:

1. Adjusting

The early years of marriage require a lot of adjustments. Change is not just about adopting or doing new things; it's also about letting go of old things that are no longer useful or rewarding.

We can change ourselves, but we can't change our partners. Your spouse can change for the better just by you changing for the best.

2. Pruning

As life gets busier, a crucial skill in marriage is prioritising our relationship (pruning back certain areas of our lives to prioritise another).

We will only survive as a couple if we learn to prioritise our marriage relationship over every other demand on our time.

3. Supporting

Marriages need a support network (from God, friends, family, and older married couples we can learn from).

We may face challenges from illness, infertility, finances, an empty nest, and elderly parent(s).

Supporting and encouraging our partner is essential.

When we support each other, the very challenges we face can draw us closer together.

4. Renewing

Being prepared to talk about our own individual needs and desires.

Sharing our hopes for our future together with our partner.

Slowing down for long enough to decide on changes we'd like to make.

Considering whether we should stop certain activities to have more time together.

Starting something new that will strengthen, restore, or renew the connection between us.

If you're struggling in your marriage, be encouraged that reconnection is possible.

When couples tend to their relationship, things can change dramatically, and they can go on to experience a new level of connection and intimacy.

A NEW EXPERIENCE STARTS WITH THE FOLLOWING TRUTHS:

MAKE TIME FOR EACH OTHER

Making time for the people that matter most in our lives doesn't just happen; it requires a conscious decision. If a relationship is to thrive and keep growing, we must have regular quality time together.

Plan a 'date day or date night' with your partner once a week—spend one to two hours or as much as you want, alone together to rekindle romance, have fun, and talk together about your feelings (your hopes, fears, worries, excitements, and memories).

CLEAN AS YOU GO

Deal with issues and offences as the occasion demands. No carryovers. Give no room for strife, bitterness, and revenge. It drains you of trust, the fun in marriage, genuine friendship, intimacy, and affection for each other. The key is to remain friends for life. Naked together and not ashamed.

NURTURE EACH OTHER

Nurturing involves seeking to meet each other's emotional needs for affection, encouragement, intimacy, support, comfort, etc.

It's as though there's an empty space inside each of us that needs to be filled up with another person's love and attention.

When we're known intimately, loved by another, and no longer alone, the space inside is filled up. The way to keep filling up this space inside is by recognising and meeting each other's emotional needs.

THE ART OF COMMUNICATION

We all have a deep longing for emotional connection; it is a fundamental human need. An emotional connection in marriage can only be achieved where there is good communication.

Effective communication

This is Engaging in good, intimate, life-changing, harmless conversation. Communicating with clarity and respecting one another with love talk is essential. Correcting in love, with moderation and consideration, and expressing our feelings, thoughts, and ideas.

Different levels of communication:

Level 1: Passing on information

Level 2: Sharing our ideas and opinions

Level 3: Being open about our feelings and needs

Level 3 includes vulnerability, requires trust, and involves both effective speaking and listening well.

Good communication is multilayered, and it involves:

- Our words

- Our tone of voice

- Our body language

THE IMPORTANCE OF LISTENING

Our aim in marriage should be to listen twice as much as we talk.

Good listening is one of the most important skills to learn for a strong marriage. Listening has great power to make our husband or wife feel loved and valued.

HINDRANCES TO LISTENING

Listening is in a class on its own and helps facilitate effective communication. It aids proper understanding and gives clarity when situations and scenarios are complicated. It's also a skill that must be developed over a period of time. However, when listening is drummed out or hindered, there are undesirable developments that arise that are not conducive to viable relationships. This complication starts with bad habits that are also developed over a period of time.

FIVE BAD LISTENING HABITS

1. Disengaging

When we have a separate conversation going on in our heads, or when we're not listening properly because of our physical environment.

2. Reassuring

Not allowing our partner to voice negative emotions.

3. Giving advice

Focusing on solutions rather than empathising with our partner.

4. Going off on a tangent

Taking over the conversation with our own agenda.

5. Interrupting

Failing to let our partner finish what they want to say.

6. Distractions

When we allow other things, such as favourite TV programmes or social media, to divert our attention.

These habits can prevent the speaker from saying what they're feeling, which may eventually cause them to shut down.

We can all learn the art of effective listening, but it takes time and requires us to be intentional about it.

FIVE STEPS FOR EFFECTIVE AND REFLECTIVE LISTENING

1. Always to put yourself in your partner's shoes.

Put your own views to one side and really appreciate what it's like for your partner to be feeling the way that they do.

2. Acknowledge what they've said.

When you have listened to what your partner wants to say, reflect on what they have said rather than putting in your own opinion or point of view.

3. Find out what is most important.

Then ask your husband or wife: 'What is the most important part of what you have been saying?'

4. Help them work out what they might do.

Now ask: 'Is there anything you would like to do (or, if appropriate, like me or us to do) about what you have said?'

15

5. Ask if your partner has said all they need to.

Don't assume you already know everything your partner wants to say. If there is more they wish to express, create space for it and listen with patience.

RESOLVING CONFLICT

Conflict is inevitable in every marriage—all couples will disagree about certain, few or many things.

We come into marriage with and from different backgrounds, desires, priorities, trainings, baggages and personalities.

It's no good trying to force our partner to do things our way.

If we have the right tools, addressing the conflict can strengthen our relationship.

In marriage, we are on the same side and never forget that we are a team.

FOUR PRINCIPLES FOR HANDLING CONFLICT

1. Remember your partner's positive qualities.

Continue to show appreciation for what you love (and admire) about your partner (even while you may disagree passionately about various issues). The more we concentrate on the things we appreciate about each other, the more appreciative we become of each other.

Make it a daily habit to appreciate your partner. Verbalise it. Journalise it. Lots of compliments. So priceless.

2. Recognise that differences are good.

Don't try to change each other. Learn to accept differences of temperament, personality, upbringing, and values.

See your marriage as a partnership in which you combine your strengths and support each other's weaknesses.

3. Look for a 'us' solution. There is no lone-ranger attraction. Together we achieve more.

4. Support your partner.

When we expect our partner to meet all our needs, we inevitably fail each other and get hurt, causing our marriage to spiral downwards.

Focus more on meeting your partner's needs rather than expecting them to meet yours.

5. Depend on God.

When we look to God to meet our needs for unconditional love, we are able to focus more easily on the needs of others.

Praying for each other helps us connect regularly {five to ten minutes a day is generally better than one hour every month}.

Ask each other, 'What can I pray about for you today?'

Draw on God's promises from the Bible and start with thankfulness.

The closer each of us is individually in our relationship with God, the nearer we will be to each other as husband and wife.

If one of you has upset the other, say sorry and forgive each other before praying. Ask your partner, 'What can I pray for you today?'

RESOLVING CONFLICTS

Five Practical Steps

a. Focus on the issue

Move the issue from between you and put it in front of you.

Discuss the issue rather than attacking each other.

b. Use of 'I' statements

Avoid labelling ('You always…', 'You never…')

Describe your feelings ('I feel undervalued when…'). Being more considerate for one another.

c. Listen to each other.

Take turns talking. Talking over one another is disrespectful, dominant, spells impatience and lack sensitivity.

d. Brainstorm possible solutions

Make a list if necessary. Reasoning together, pulling wisdom resources together, deliberating and avoiding rioting. Two are better than one for they have good rewards for their labour.

e. Decide on the best solution for now and review later.

If it's not working, try another solution from your list. Invent and reinvent, don't be tied up or locked down or bound to liberalism, customs and traditions. There are no fast rules or shortcuts to arrive at all endpoints or conclusions.

NB: Take an issue that's causing conflict and adapt with these 'ABOVE' five steps.

THE POWER OF FORGIVENESS

Saying sorry and forgiving each other are vital because we will all hurt our partners at some point.

Unresolved hurt will undermine the trust and openness between us, destroying our intimacy.

REACTIONS TO HURT

- Anger

First and foremost, anger on its own is not bad in itself if channeled rightly. It has a God-given purpose and is part of our internal mechanism for signalling that something is wrong and needs to be sorted out.

On the other hand, anger is ugly and cruel if applied in a negative way when emotions run high and uncontrollable leading to hurts, pains and devastations.

What happens if hurt and anger are buried inside? Let's check out the symptoms:

Behavioural Symptoms

1. Inability to relax

2. Low sexual desire

3. Quick temper/intolerance

4. Escape through drugs, alcohol, pornography, etc.

5. Escape into work/children/religious activities and sports, etc.

Physical Symptoms

1. Disturbed sleep

2. Appetite affected

3. Medical conditions, such as ulcers, high blood pressure, cancer and protracted pain & aches.

Emotional Symptoms

1. Loss of positive emotions such as romance, love, and joy

2. Low self-esteem/depression

3. Emotional Shut down

4. Fear of confrontation

Social Symptoms

1. Withdrawal from public sceneries

2. Jumping into wrong conclusions

3. Little or no participation in peculiar occasions.

4. Poor judgement of people and situations.

PROCESSES FOR HEALING HURT

1. Talk about the hurt.

Whether you have hurt your spouse or have been hurt by them, take the initiative to bring it out into the open so things can be deliberated on to experience healing. An accumulation of small hurts, if left unaddressed, can lead to a loss of intimacy, just as small stones can eventually block a drain.

2. Say sorry.

Take responsibility—resist the urge to make excuses or to blame your partner.

Making excuses/blaming our partner: 'I know I criticised you in front of the children yesterday, but I wouldn't have done so if you hadn't made us late.'

Proper apology: 'I hurt you by criticising you in front of the children yesterday; it was unkind of me. I'm sorry.'

Confessing our faults to God and receiving His forgiveness helps us to see how our actions have hurt our partner.

3. Forgive for real at all cost.

Forgiveness is essential and one of the greatest forces for healing in a marriage.

Forgiveness is, first and foremost, a choice, not a feeling.

Forgiveness always costs us something. The question is not, 'Do we feel like forgiving?' but, 'Will we forgive? Will we let go of our self-pity/demand for justice/desire to retaliate?'

FORGIVENESS IS NOT:

1. Pretending that the hurt doesn't matter and trying to forget about it.

2. Denying the hurt (and just hoping it will go away).

3. Thinking, 'Our love for each other will somehow magically resolve any way we hurt each other, so it doesn't matter'.

Forgiveness IS:

1. Facing the wrong done to us

2. Recognising the emotions inside

3. Choosing not to hold it against our partner

Forgiveness is a process. We often need to keep forgiving for the same hurt, sometimes on a daily basis.

FEW REASONS TO FORGIVE:

- To free us from anger and bitterness
- To allow us to live in our divine design
- To free up space for our health and peace
- To release us from the torment of the issue
- To free us to be effective in the present
- To ensure that God will hear and answer our prayers

THE IMPACT OF FAMILY

Family background has a big influence on a marriage. Two families always come together to form a third brand new family, hence three different marriages. Therefore the three families become and are supposed to be ONE family in all dimensions.

For some people, the support they receive from their family is good and helpful in building a strong marriage.

For others, their wider family dynamics are more complicated and can even be damaging.

LEAVING AND LETTING GO

When we get married, a profound positive change should take place in our relationship with our parents (or whoever was our primary carer during our upbringing).

The transition from being a child and completely dependent on them to achieving healthy independence as an adult is most unique.

The significance of leaving is not so much the physical move as the psychological and emotional one.

We create a new 'centre of gravity'—our highest loyalty must be to our spouse.

SUPPORT EACH OTHER

If necessary, put boundaries in place and don't cut yourself off from your parents, but instead connect with them as a couple in a new and better way.

Listen to parental advice, but make your own decisions together as a couple with God's direction and instructions.

BUILDING HEALTHY MARITAL RELATIONSHIPS

1. Resolve any conflict.

Unblock the drain:

Identify and discuss the main issue causing tension, and apologise when you have been wrong. Choose to forgive and move on.

2. Consider their needs.

It can be helpful to take the initiative with parents about things like:

- Visiting them.
- Enabling them to see their grandchildren.
- Working out what holidays you might spend together.
- Getting in touch with them regularly.

3. Looking at our past

We bring a mixture of experiences into our marriage from our family background:

- What was good (be grateful for that).
- What was different from our partner's experience (be aware that this can cause conflict).
- What was negative (and may be painful).

HEALING CHILDHOOD PAIN

1. Grieve your own and your partner's unmet needs.

You may encounter strong feelings as you do this, but recognising and admitting to yourself the hurt you've experienced can be a huge step forward. Allow your partner to talk about what they suffered or missed out on and give them the gift of your emotional support.

2. Forgive.

Give up continuing to hold onto expectations and longings for what you have wanted your parents or others to be for you. Remember, forgiveness is an ongoing act of the will and is essential for healing.

Forgiving someone is not condoning their actions or giving them the right to repeat what they've done. Forgiveness is about being set free from the ways they've hurt you.

SECRETS FOR KEEPING THE ROMANTIC FLAME ALIVE AND STRENGTHENING INTIMACY IN MARRIAGE

1. SPEAKING

Difficult at first because our sexuality is deeply private and requires vulnerability.

Tell each other what you enjoy—don't leave it to guesswork.

Don't regard any issues in your sexual relationship as 'your' issue or 'my' issue, but 'our' issue.

2. PRIORITISING

Guard the physical space for your lovemaking.

Be creative:

- Avoid the drive-through mentality and focus on intimacy.
- The atmosphere—soft lighting can help.
- The 'how' you make love.
- Who takes the initiative
- Approach variety with sensitivity at a mutually agreeable pace.

Our attitude should be to seek to give pleasure to our partner and not just take it for ourselves.

Sex isn't just the icing on the cake of a marriage—it's an important ingredient of the cake itself.

3. ANTICIPATING

Our most potent and important sexual asset is our mind.

Having your own private language and private signals around sex sparks thoughts that create anticipation and build desire.

Mutually agreed-upon periods of sexual abstinence can enhance a couple's sexual relationship.

Romance creates the setting for lovemaking.

Be sure sexual thoughts and desires are directed towards your partner and not someone else, which can lead to emotional adultery.

Romance is the bridge between the everyday world of practicality and the private place of our sexual relationship.

4. RESPONDING

Sex often starts as a decision, and then arousal follows.

Giving ourselves sexually requires a climate of trust.

Responding sexually can give our spouse a sense of confidence and well-being.

5. KINDNESS

Sex is about giving—showing support in practical ways and taking time to tune in to each other's emotional needs.

Men and women are wired differently when it comes to sexual arousal.

Our kind words will build confidence in our partner.

Don't criticise your spouse's natural shape.

Tell each other what you love about their body and what makes it unique.

There is a very strong link between building each other's self-esteem and building an intimate sexual relationship.

6. SATISFACTION

Enjoying your spouse is essential, instead of enduring them.

7. GOOD SEX

Emotional connection creates good sex, and good sex creates a greater emotional connection.

Sex is the ultimate body language through which we communicate our desire for our spouse or desire for:

- Closeness
- Comfort
- Love expressions
- Protection
- Procreation (children bearing)

Our sexual relationship:

- Restores our emotional well-being, which helps us cope with the pressures of life.
- Expresses and deepens the 'one flesh' bond.

LOVE IN ACTION

Love is about more than feelings; it's about what we do—it involves action. Love always costs us something.

THE FIVE LOVE LANGUAGES

1. Loving words

2. Thoughtful presents

3. Physical affection

4. Quality time

5. Kind actions

For each of us, one of these 'love languages' will communicate love more effectively than the others.

Most people have different love languages from their partners.

Often, we try to communicate love in the way we understand it and want to receive it.

A marriage that is full of love is where we are seeking to meet our husband or wife's needs in a particular way that makes them feel loved.

1. Loving words

Words have great power, either to build up or to tear down our partner.

Give compliments and encourage each other daily.

Speak kindly to each other.

For some people, hearing words of affirmation feels like arriving at an oasis in a desert.

2. Thoughtful presents

Giving presents is a way of investing in our marriage.

Presents can be expensive or inexpensive, but they often have high value; for example, a single flower or a bar of chocolate.

Please don't wait only for special occasions.

Actively discover what your partner likes (within your budget!).

3. Physical affection

Affectionate touch is a powerful communicator of love in marriage. If this is your partner's primary way of feeling loved, in times of crisis, touch will communicate more than anything else that you care.

We need to use the whole range and find out from our partner what's appropriate at different moments: holding hands, putting an arm round each other's shoulder or waist, a kiss, a hug, a hand on a hand, a back massage, sexual foreplay, and making love.

4. Quality time

Togetherness means more than physical proximity. It involves focusing our attention on our partner.

Quality time together builds friendship through:

- Talking together
- Eating together
- Having fun together

5. Kind actions

This involves expressing love through serving our partner and seeking to meet their needs in practical ways.

Find out from your partner what kind of actions are most meaningful for them.

Love is not just a feeling—it requires an act of the will to meet each other's needs. We are called to imitate the love of Jesus.

Chapter Two

DESTRUCTIVE HABITS IN MARRIAGE

EMOTIONAL AFFAIR

Emotional affairs start with a confusing web of mixed feelings, flirtations, building fantasies, and mentally planning out a new life with someone not your spouse. It leads to deception and threatens to sabotage your marriage.

Couples have to be VERY careful about having close friends of the opposite sex, because most affairs start as "friendships" that cross the line.

If you think that you (or your spouse) have let a friendship go too far, here are a few simple ways to tell if you're having some level of an emotional affair. If you can see yourself in any of these, take immediate action to create healthy boundaries and restore healing and trust in your marriage.

"Flee all appearances of evil….."

SIGNS OF AN EMOTIONAL AFFAIR:

1. You're having conversations you wouldn't want your spouse to see.

If you're ever in a position where you think, "I'm glad my husband/wife isn't seeing this," then you're already out of bounds, and you're playing with fire. A healthy marriage requires complete trust and transparency.

2. You're dressing to impress a specific individual other than your spouse.

When we try to be visually attractive to someone other than our spouse, we're opening a very dangerous door. Wanting to be professional and look your best is one thing, but wanting to look your best for one specific person is something else entirely.

3. You try to create opportunities to be alone with someone other than your spouse.

If you're going out of your way to "run into" someone so you can have one-on-one conversations, that's a huge red flag. You need to put immediate distance between you and him/her.

4. You delete text messages or emails from someone because you don't want your spouse to see them.

If you're ever hiding messages, texts or calls, then you've crossed an obvious line and you're having an emotional affair.

5. You're having consistent romantic or sexual fantasies about someone other than your spouse.

Affairs don't start in the bedroom; they always start in the mind! If you allow your mind to play out fantasies, you're giving a piece of your heart to the object of that fantasy, and you're opening the door for the fantasy to become a reality.

6. You're constantly mentally or otherwise comparing your spouse to this other individual.

When you become emotionally involved with someone, the mental tendency is to see this new person as nearly flawless, and, by comparison, your spouse's flaws become much more obvious. If you're more critical of your spouse while mentally comparing them to this other person, you're falling into a toxic trap.

JAMES 1:13 KJV – *Let no man say when he is tempted, I am tempted of God: for God cannot be tempted with evil, neither tempteth he any man.*

7. You're planning a new life together with this other person.

Once you start planning and romanticising a new life with this other person, you're in a very dangerous place. I urge you to reconsider your actions and confess to your spouse. Fight for your marriage!

HABITS THAT LEAD TO ADULTERY & HOW TO STOP IT NOW

Adultery in marriage doesn't just happen out of nowhere. It starts with inappropriate and sexually explicit text message exchanges with another person who's not your spouse. This subconsciously pulls you away from your spouse emotionally and physically because you are giving more and more thought to this other strange person.

In this particular instance, no physical/sexual lines were crossed before the emotional affair came to light, but even still, great damage had already been done to the marriage. Like so many couples, they have found themselves in a place they never expected to be, and now they're starting the process of rebuilding trust and trying to restore their relationship.

These traits below aren't specifically related to an inappropriate relationship with someone that could lead to adultery in marriage, BUT these actions seem to create a mindset in your marriage where adultery is much more likely to happen.

1. Criticising your spouse in public, private, or online.

The tone of your words will shape the tone of your marriage. Criticism, nagging, or constantly "correcting" your spouse can make both you and your spouse more vulnerable to an affair. When you look at your spouse with a critical eye, you're more likely to have your eyes open to someone else, and your spouse is more likely to be drawn in by someone who will compliment them instead of criticising. If there's a climate of criticism in your marriage, take immediate action to change it. Be your spouse's biggest encourager, not their biggest critic!

2. Lack of physical affection could lead to adultery in marriage.

If you and your spouse aren't hugging, kissing, holding hands, etc., that's a big warning sign. Frequent sexual intimacy is obviously important as well, but these smaller acts of everyday physical touch are so important to the physical and emotional connectedness that keeps a husband and wife bonded. If your marriage is lacking in this area, start initiating physical contact. If your spouse doesn't receive your advances with warmth, start conversations about the reasons for the disconnection. A marriage starved of sex and other forms of physical affection is in a dangerous and vulnerable place.

3. Surrounding ourselves with friends who don't know (or don't like) your spouse.

I'm convinced that one of the biggest factors that leads people into affairs is the friends they choose to hang around. This might sound surprising to you, but I've seen it play out over and over. In most (not all) cases of adultery in marriage, the spouse who had the affair had also been spending time with friends or co-workers who don't encourage marital faithfulness. Surround yourself with friends who strengthen your character and distance yourself from those who attempt to compromise it.

4. Stubborn Pride (Believing your way is always the right way or the only way).

When you start disrespecting your spouse by belittling his/her viewpoints, you're opening the door for infidelity.

Pride is that sinister little whisper in your ear, making you feel entitled to do everything your way and in your preferred timing. Pride destroys relationships more than anything else. Show mutual respect at all times. Respect and thoughtfulness aren't just good tools for preventing adultery in marriage. They are vital to health in every part of your marriage. Just because your spouse does things differently from you doesn't necessarily mean your way is better (or worse). Celebrate each other's differences.

5. Keeping secrets from your spouse.

Secrecy is the enemy of intimacy.

The moment you start deleting text messages, hiding things or doing anything you hope your spouse doesn't find out about, you're already way out of line! If you want your marriage to thrive and be protected from adultery, make the "Secret-Free Guarantee." Never keep secrets and never tell lies to your spouse. Full and transparent honesty is the only way a marriage can work.

6. Threatening divorce could lead to adultery in marriage.

Screaming divorce threats in marriage can shatter the foundation of trust that every marriage should be built upon. Whenever we start creating exit strategies in our minds or whenever we threaten to leave, it creates an atmosphere where infidelity (and many other negative factors) can more easily occur. The strongest marriages remove all exit strategies and remove the word "divorce" from their vocabularies.

7. Going on "autopilot" (when you stop making efforts to strengthen your marriage).

We've all been around couples where one or both spouses have "checked out" of the relationship. They still live in the same house, and technically, they are still married, but their thoughts and hearts might as well be a thousand miles away. They've grown numb, and they've silently given up even trying to make things better. If this (or any of the factors on this list) is happening in your marriage, please don't lose hope and don't fall for the toxic temptation of having an affair. There is help and hope available for your marriage. Get counselling. Get help. Don't give up.

RUINING A MARRIAGE

Many people today are unknowingly doing great damage and more harm than good to their marriage. Some always blame the devil or some members of their spouse's family.

WAYS PEOPLE RUIN THEIR MARRIAGE

1. Keeping scores

These are the marriages where one or both spouses are always "keeping score" of the other spouse's behaviour and then using that information to manipulate or control aspects of the marriage. Forgiveness is never truly sought or truly given. Scorekeepers always have their guard up because they view marriage as a contest to be won against their spouse instead of something to be won in partnership with their spouse.

2. Living in Fantasy

These couples have nearly given up on pursuing passionate intimacy with each other, so they often escape into fantasy through romance novels or porn. The deeper they go into the fantasy, the more desensitised they become to real love and the more unsatisfied they become with their spouse, sex life, and marriage.

3. Outsourcing and role-playing

These dysfunctional couples take the most sacred aspects of marriage (emotional support, friendship, acceptance, companionship, and sometimes even sex) and "outsource" those roles to other people or pursuits. They may also find fulfilment in their career or hobbies if they discover it in those arenas. They give the best of themselves to other people or pursuits at the expense of their marriage.

4. Blame games

These are the marriages where one or both spouses consistently blame the other for all the struggles in the marriage. These couples tend to have regular arguments (often heated) with no real resolutions. Even when they are not arguing, their communication still contains a great deal of sarcasm and nagging. They live in perpetual frustration with each other.

5. Married but still single

These are the couples who never seem to fully grasp the partnership required for a healthy marriage. They live as two separate individuals with separate hopes, dreams, money (often separate bank accounts, not that there's anything wrong with that), hobbies, friends, and eventually, separate lives altogether.

6. Deception and lack of trust

These couples have no trust in each other, and their lack of trust is perpetuated by keeping secrets and hiding details (or hiding money, conversations, etc.) from each other. Without trust and transparency in marriage, couples live in a state of artificial harmony, and they never experience true intimacy, because secrecy is an enemy of intimacy.

7. Sitting on the Fence approach

These are the couples who hit the "snooze button" on their issues instead of actually dealing with them. They might be aware of issues in the relationship, but it doesn't feel urgent, so it becomes more comfortable to ignore them until they worsen. They secretly hope that their passive approach will resolve the problems and that they will go away on their own, but it doesn't work that way.

8. Giving Up Mentality

These couples throw around the word "divorce" in nearly every disagreement until they finally follow through and give up on the marriage. They see struggles in marriage as an excuse to quit, rather than an opportunity to work together and grow stronger with their spouse. They very often remarry someone else and then repeat the same cycles of dysfunction in the new relationship.

SPOUSE TREATMENT

HOW TO TREAT YOUR SPOUSE

1. Don't shout at your spouse when you are talking. It really hurts them.

A soft answer turns away wrath, But a harsh word stirs up anger (**PROVERBS 15:1; NKJV**).

2. Do not speak evil of them to anyone. Your spouse will become who you call them.

Out of the ground the Lord God formed every beast of the field and every bird of the air, and brought them to Adam to see what he would call them. And whatever Adam called each living creature, that was its name (**GENESIS 2:19; NKJV**).

3. Do not share their love or affection with someone else. It is called adultery.

But I say to you that whoever looks at a woman to lust for her has already committed adultery with her in his heart (Matthew 5:28; NKJV).

4. Never compare your spouse to somebody else. If the other woman or the other man were good for you, God would have given them to you.

For we dare not class ourselves or compare ourselves with those who commend themselves. But they, measuring themselves by themselves, and comparing themselves among themselves, are not wise (**II CORINTHIANS 10:12; NKJV**).

5. Be gentle and accommodating. He or she has sacrificed so much to be with you. It hurts deeply when you are harsh and irritating. Be tender.

With all lowliness and gentleness, with longsuffering, bearing with one another in love (**EPHESIANS 4:2; NKJV**).

6. Hide nothing from your spouse. You are now one and a helpmate. Let there be no secret you are keeping from them.

And they were both naked, the man and his wife, and were not ashamed (**GENESIS 2:25; NKJV**).

7. Do not make negative comments about your wife's body. She risked her life and beauty to carry your babies. She is a living soul, not just flesh and blood.

He who finds a wife finds a good thing, And obtains favor from the Lord (**PROVERBS 18:22; NKJV**).

8. Do not let your spouse's body determine their worth. Cherish and appreciate each other even till old age.

For no one ever hated his own flesh, but nourishes and cherishes it, just as the Lord does the church (**EPHESIANS 5:29; NKJV**).

9. Never shout at each other in public or private. If you have an issue to sort with them, do it in the privacy of your room.

Then Joseph, her husband, being a just man, and not wanting to make her a public example, was minded to put her away secretly (**MATTHEW 1:19; NKJV**)

10. Thank and appreciate your spouse for taking good care of you, the children and the house. It is a great sacrifice being made.

In everything give thanks; for this is the will of God in Christ Jesus for you (**I THESSALONIANS 5:18; NKJV**).

11. All women cannot cook the same way; appreciate your wife's food. (Not all husbands can do home DIY, etc.). Appreciate even the little he's doing.

It is not easy to cook three meals a day, 365 days a year, for several years.

She is like the merchant ships, She brings her food from afar (**PROVERBS 31:14; NKJV**).

12. Never place your siblings before your spouse. You're a companion for life and one together. Your spouse must come before your family.

Therefore a man shall leave his father and mother and be joined to his wife, and they shall become one flesh (**GENESIS 2:24; NKJV**).

13. Invest seriously in their spiritual growth. Buy books, tapes, and any other materials that will edify & strengthen their walk with God. That's the best thing you can do for them.

That He might sanctify and cleanse her with the washing of water by the word (**EPHESIANS 5:26; NKJV**).

14. Spend time together doing Bible study and praying.

Confess your trespasses to one another, and pray for one another, that you may be healed. The effective, fervent prayer of a righteous man avails much (**JAMES 5:16; NKJV**).

15. Make time to play with your spouse and enjoy their company. Remember, when you are dead, he or she is the one who will be by your grave because your friends may be too busy to attend your funeral.

Live joyfully with the wife whom you love all the days of your vain life which He has given you under the sun, all your days of vanity; for that is your portion in life, and in the labor which you perform under the sun (**ECCLESIASTES 9:9; NKJV**).

16. Never use money to manipulate or control your spouse. Remember, you nurse each other with your possessions till death do you part. You're joint heirs together by the grace of God.

Husbands, likewise, dwell with them with understanding, giving honor to the wife, as to the weaker vessel, and as being heirs together of the grace of life, that your prayers may not be hindered (**I PETER 3:7; NKJV**).

17. Do not expose your spouse's weakness. You will be exposing yourself too. Be a shield around one another.

For we are members of His body, of His flesh and of His bones (**EPHESIANS 5:30; NKJV**).

18. Honour your spouse's parents and be kind to their siblings.

I would lead you and bring you into the house of my mother, She who used to instruct me. I would cause you to drink of spiced wine, Of the juice of my pomegranate (**SONG OF SOLOMON 8:2; NKJV**).

19. Never cease to tell your spouse how much you love them for the rest of their life. Women are never tired of hearing that. Men also love compliments.

Husbands, love your wives, just as Christ also loved the church and gave Himself for her (**EPHESIANS 5:25; NKJV**).

20. Grow to be like Jesus. That's the only way you can be a good and a godly spouse.

For whom He foreknew, He also predestined to be conformed to the image of His Son, that He might be the firstborn among many brethren (**ROMANS 8:29; NKJV**).

WAYS TO SHOW YOUR WIFE RESPECT

The truth is that both men and women need respect (and love), but that need is manifested in different ways.

Each marriage is unique (because each person is unique), so this list may not represent all people. The point of this section isn't to squeeze everyone into the same mould, but rather to spark meaningful dialogue between husbands and wives, which will ultimately lead to stronger marriages.

Ways a wife needs respect from her husband:

1. Have eyes only for her.

A man shows respect for his wife by never making her feel compared to an airbrushed supermodel or a random woman passing by. Men make their wives feel safe, adored, and respected when their eyes are "monogamous."

2. Support and encourage her dreams.

A man shows respect for his wife when her dreams become his priority. In both big and small things, men should encourage and support their wives to achieve their hopes and dreams.

3. Work hard to provide for the family.

When a man works hard, it communicates respect to his wife. A lazy man is incapable of communicating true respect to his wife (or anyone else).

4. Help out around the house.

Each household is different, but in the homes where the wife manages the domestic duties, the husband should still be willing to jump in and help out. Doing the dishes or folding laundry is a simple way to show your wife respect.

5. Engage in conversation with her and listen when she is talking.

I believe the typical wife's need for communication is every bit as strong as the typical husband's need for sex. A husband shows respect to his wife when he turns off his phone, turns off the TV, and engages in meaningful conversation. He ALWAYS tells her the truth. Dishonesty is the ultimate form of disrespect.

6. Make time with your wife a priority.

A man shows respect for his wife when he makes her a constant priority on his calendar. A husband should give his best energies to his wife, not his leftovers after he has given his best to hobbies, a career, or other pursuits.

7. Continuously pursues her.

Most guys are great at pursuing the lady during the dating phase of a relationship, but we often become lazy, inconsistent, and unromantic in marriage. We show our love and respect to our wives by continuously giving them the best of ourselves and by continually growing better together with every season of life.

8. Never give up on her!

Love means believing in someone even when they struggle to believe in themselves. Do this for your wife. Bring out the best in her. Build her up through your words, actions, and respect. Let her know that your commitment to her and your love for her are unconditional and unshakeable. That will give her the confidence to take on the world, knowing you always have her back!

Chapter Three

MAKING GOOD MARITAL CHOICES

CHOICES COUPLES MAKE

1. MARRIAGE IS ABOUT CHOICE

The big idea behind the transformation of your marriage is that you can make choices in key areas to heal it. You are in control of the conflicts that occur in your relationship. Conflict, in and of itself, is not a bad thing. What is important is how we deal with it. Conflicts will happen, but fights don't have to. You can make different choices. The first major choice both of you must make is to stop doing what has not worked in your relationship so far.

Before you say this is oversimplifying marriage, think about it. Isn't stopping what you're doing wrong the exact place where you have to start? You have to learn what doesn't work in your relationship and make a clear choice not to do that anymore. That is the only way to make space and try new ways of handling problems.

The second choice to make is deciding if you are willing to work together as a team instead of competing against each other to achieve your own individual goals. You can choose to do what your partner needs and give up what you need.

> You can choose to forgive your spouse even when you don't feel your partner deserves forgiveness.

2. MARRIAGE IS ALSO ABOUT HOPE

There is hope that if you have made poor choices in the past, you can adopt a different approach in the future. There is hope that your relationship and your future as a couple are not at the mercy of disagreements or conflict. There is hope that the marriage you believed in when you said "I do" is not only possible but within your reach. And there is room for hope even if hope never existed.

With so many hurting people and damaged marriages, I can't emphasise enough that your marriage is not hopeless, and you are not helpless. Your relationship doesn't have to continue on the way it is. You can choose to start making choices that will transform your marriage. You will learn how to understand the process of what happens when you and your partner are in conflict and how to focus more on the way you treat each other than on what you disagree about.

> What area of your marriage, if restored, would give you a sense of hope? Take a small step in that direction.

3. CHOOSE TO FOCUS ON THE PROCESS

As we discussed earlier, conflict is not inherently bad. What is important is how we deal with it. One of the biggest myths about marriage is that fights "just happen"; that they are random and unpredictable events. Instead, I believe that people make a conscious, deliberate choice when they decide to turn a disagreement into a fight. The success of a marriage is often seen in how a couple handles conflict with each other.

Couples must be open to feedback from each other, strive to become the most authentic and loving partners possible, and learn to bring real and lasting transformation to their marriage. In working with couples, it's believed that process matters much more than content. A difference in beliefs or attitudes about a certain topic does not necessarily create conflict between partners, as most couples can work through differences of opinion. The way couples treat each other when discussing issues often causes greater conflict. In fact, many couples, when they learn to focus on treating each other with respect, honour, and love, sometimes don't even remember what they were arguing about!

To this end, we need to understand what is meant when we talk about processes. This is the way two people interact within their marriage, how they treat one another, and what happens between them that drives the behaviours they choose to display. Process focuses on how you relate to each other. In contrast, content focuses on what you disagree on every day—the specific issues that create difficulty, such as parenting, work, or in-laws.

People in a relationship need to start thinking differently about conflicts between them and their partner. Instead of thinking about conflict in terms of what you fight about, think about how you treat each other during an argument. For example, what are your attitudes and behaviours like? Are you mean and hurtful, or do you show respect, love, and honour to each other? Do you interrupt and criticise each other, or do you listen well and focus on your partner?

Learning to make these choices will not be easy, and overcoming the potential challenges to your relationship will not be a painless process. You didn't arrive where you are overnight, so you won't build the marriage of your dreams overnight either. The hope you can believe in is that you and your partner can choose to be in control of what happens in your relationship. If you have the courage to take this journey, the possibilities are life-changing.

> You are responsible for the choices you make within your marriage. Does that statement feel empowering or defeating? Why?

4. CHOOSE TO LISTEN

Changing how you speak to each other, when you speak to each other, and where you speak to each other are important for building success in your marriage. Focusing on how you both feel rather than winning the argument and listening to your partner so that you truly understand what they want you to know are equally valuable choices. These choices can prevent the anger and resentment so many couples experience.

In the past, you may have felt enlightened for educating yourself on the rules of fighting fairly in conflicts. Couples will have disagreements. You don't need to "fight fair," but not fight at all! Positive communication will cause a shift in the direction of wholeness.

So, what does positive communication look like?

Positive communication focuses on what is currently happening at present.

It does not bring up the past and create a negative atmosphere by reinstating old emotions.

It focuses on one clear issue at a time. Honest communication doesn't muddy the waters with different issues that are sensitive and emotional. Stay on task.

Additionally, be aware that the right setting is crucial for proper communication. Productive discourse occurs when both parties have energy, clarity, and focus. Therefore, trying to communicate at the end of the day when you are tired is not a good plan for discussing something confrontational with your spouse.

Don't choose the heat of the moment to drive your point home or try to hide the truth, either. That choice has harmful consequences, and you are learning to maintain a positive and honest approach.

Choosing to be resilient in your relationship involves more than communication. Couples who function from a positive mindset are more cooperative than competitive. When the relationship becomes competitive, it has likely also turned negative.

In contrast, a healthy marriage is a cooperative venture in which both partners strive to help each other become the best individuals and spouses they can be. The goal is not to win by accumulating more of the limited resources in the relationship but to ensure that each partner is loved, accepted, valued, and honoured in their interactions.

> Is winning the argument more important to you than showing compassion toward your spouse? The next time you start to argue, intentionally choose to stop and listen to your spouse's perspective. What happened when you did?

5. CHOOSE TO GET RID OF BAGGAGE

The intent of today is to help you understand some of the relationship patterns you may have brought into your marriage from your childhood and your previous relationships. With knowledge of these patterns, you can learn positive strategies and stop using ineffective ones. Learning to change old patterns involves recognising where you are in the process and getting out of it.

The patterns from the past, whether they come from your childhood or previous relationships, were successful and useful when you developed them. These behaviours and patterns helped you cope with the challenges you faced at those times. However, they may no longer be effective if the reasons you used them do not exist in your current marriage.

In creating a healthy process of handling conflict in your marriage, one of the most effective parenting interventions is the timeout. When a child's behaviour gets out of control or parents need to change the direction of a child's behaviour, they have the child take a timeout. The same principle can work wonders for your marital relationship. The goal is to learn how to work together to effectively disengage when your interactions are not healthy.

Either one of you can call for a timeout, but you both need to commit to honouring the request when it is made. Additionally, you both agree to let go of your desire to win the fight and trust that taking a break is best for both parties. Simply agreeing to table the fight for the time being is far better than saying or doing hurtful things. The important thing here is not to use the timeout as an excuse to avoid the conflict. The partner who requests the timeout should inform the other partner when they think it might be okay to discuss the issue again. I cannot overstate the importance of learning to take these timeouts.

By considering the baggage you both bring to the relationship from your families of origin and past relationships, you'll understand why some of the patterns in your relationship occur. Something as simple (but not easy) as taking a timeout is a learnt tool that provides clear steps for changing hurtful patterns within your marriage.

> Honour your spouse when they ask for a timeout in the middle of an argument. How did that feel, to put their need to 'pause' ahead of your need to continue with the argument?

6. CHOOSE TO CHALLENGE UNSPOKEN TRUTHS

Some of the most insidious and destructive elements of a marriage are the assumptions spouses make about each other. Assumptions are sometimes based on previous experiences that have been interpreted and, at other times, are based on minimal factual information. They are beliefs that have been adopted and later become an integral part of the reality of the relationship.

The problem with assumptions is that they become "unspoken truths." These are assumptions, which may or may not be true, that are accepted as truth in a marriage. Once accepted, partners give up trying to change these beliefs. These "unspoken truths" form the basis for how spouses act toward each other and drive much of what happens in the relationship. Once spouses begin to accept these beliefs as givens in the relationship, they become the building blocks for their understanding of each other.

Can you identify with any of the "unspoken truths" below?

- He cares more about his work than he does about me.
- She changed when we had kids; they have always been more important than me.
- He won't ever change—that's just who he is.
- No matter what I do, she'll never really love me.

- He says he works all those hours for us, but I think it's really to prove something to himself.

- I think he likes the idea of marriage, but just not the reality of being married to me.

I have seen couples find hope in the transformation that happens when they are willing to do the work of exposing "unspoken truths" in their marriages. Something powerful happens when spouses are willing to risk vulnerability with one another, speak their hurt, and put their partner first in their marriage. The same can be true for you in your marriage.

If you begin to identify the assumptions in your relationship and honestly share these "unspoken truths" with each other, you can make a clear choice to live your life together differently.

So many couples discover that they allow their entire marriage to be based on assumptions and beliefs, most of which are not true at all. When we make the brave choice to challenge these "unspoken truths" and no longer believe them, our relationship undergoes a drastic change. It may be overwhelming at first, but eventually, this choice leads to healing and truth.

> Complete these sentences with as much honesty and accuracy as possible, with the intent to share with your spouse:

My partner does not understand that I need _____.

If I could change one part of myself for my partner, it would be _____.

7. CHOOSE TO TRUST

Trust is one of the biggest challenges many couples face. Some have experienced betrayal in their marriage due to infidelity, lying, or other conflicts. Here is the thing about trust. It takes a long time to build, but it can be destroyed in an instant. Trust is the bedrock of every marriage relationship.

There are four primary conditions under which trust can grow and flourish in a marriage.

First, trust starts with honesty.

Some may lie to protect someone's feelings, out of guilt, to avoid a conflict, or to prevent others from seeing the real them. But people probably lie most often because they are worried about what will happen if they tell the truth.

If you have tried to be honest in your relationship but that attempt has been met with anger or hurtfulness, you may be hesitant to be honest in the future. You are not doing your partner any favours by allowing their emotional reaction to prevent you from being honest. Having difficult conversations shows your spouse that you care about a truly authentic relationship.

Second, trust demands integrity.

If you want to be a person of integrity in your marriage, you have to stand for something. Choose your moral code carefully, as your decisions will flow out of those principles. If you are a person of integrity, your partner will know you will honour your promises, and this is a huge step towards building trust in a marriage.

Third, trust demands reliability.

Reliability is the dependable, consistent, and steadfast application of principles such as honesty and integrity over the long haul and in all types of situations. We are talking about having each other's backs here. When your partner needs you, you are there. If you choose to value your partner over yourself, then being a partner who is reliable, honest, and a person of integrity makes complete sense.

Fourth, being vulnerable builds trust.

The last building block for a solid foundation of trust for your marriage is vulnerability. This involves allowing your spouse to get close to you and believing that they will be there for you when needed. Choosing to be vulnerable is risky—you can and often do get hurt. However, vulnerability is a step toward your partner and provides the opportunity for your spouse to make the right choice and be there when you need support, to actually come through for you.

> Which building block of trust is most difficult for you to practice? Why?

8. CHOOSE TO FORGIVE

Because of the necessity to forgive one another in any relationship, let's see what forgiveness entails.

There are four steps that couples need to learn in order to forgive one another. They are essential elements in the developmental process of forgiveness.

Step 1

An authentic apology is the first step in the process of forgiveness and involves trying to understand why you offended the other person. It also involves making a real effort to prevent it from happening again. Making a sincere apology is an ongoing process that requires commitment and follow-through. But I caution you against apologising when you don't mean it. Apologise only when you mean it—when you believe that what you did was wrong and you want to put in the work to prevent doing it again.

Step 2

Second, the process of forgiveness involves repentance. You have to show your partner that you are truly remorseful for your actions and that you have a plan in place to prevent a repeat performance in the future. This gives your apology some weight. If you don't show remorse for your actions along with a clear desire to create lasting change in yourself, you don't give your partner any reason to believe you won't do the same thing again in the future.

Step 3

Accountability is the third step because it involves both parties setting some expectations for the future. However, accountability involves more than holding each other responsible for making changes. It is also about developing a plan for success that clearly identifies all the factors that contributed to what happened. This includes both partners, as one partner's behaviour may influence the ability of the other to make the necessary changes.

Step 4

Lastly, accepting the apology of your partner means you are convinced that they feel true remorse for what they did and are working hard to prevent it from happening again. As a caution, you should not offer forgiveness unless you are honestly willing to let go of resentment and bitterness and treat the person as if the act hadn't happened. You have to believe that your partner is capable of change and expect them to succeed in that endeavour. This is much harder to do than you might think. It is much easier to protect yourself by expecting your partner to fail than to open yourself up to future pain by expecting success.

> When was the last time you showed true remorse for a wrong you had committed toward another? Was their response one of compassion or judgement?

Chapter Four

CHOOSING YOUR SPOUSE

We must possess and look out for the presence of personal traits in people in order to choose rightly, which invariably increases the chances of living together successfully.

TRAITS SUCH AS BELOW:

Ability to adjust

Being able to adjust to a relationship is called adaptability, which is a stronger trait to make relationships work than compatibility only. Compatibility focuses on the number of things you have in common. It is necessary, but there'll still be differences between you.

Adaptability, on the other hand, is your ability to adjust to each other, regardless of your differences. So, the differences wouldn't be a problem, unlike those focusing on compatibility.

Sensitivity to people's needs

Empathy is sensitivity to the needs, hurts, and desires of others—the ability to feel with them and experience the world from their perspective. Love and marriage are a relationship of meeting the needs of the other. If one or both of you aren't sensitive to the needs of the other person, there'll be so much dissatisfaction in the union.

Solving problems together

Claiming to be able to solve every problem is a lie. However, a successful marriage is comprised of a couple who have decided and remain committed to solving as many problems together as they can and finding their way around the ones they can't. But you must never pretend problems don't exist or neglect them.

Law of give and take

This is especially important for males. Most females don't have problems giving and receiving love. But males are pressured by society into believing they must remain tough and hide their emotional needs. While you both must give love, you must also receive love from the other person.

Controlling your emotions

This means being able to control your emotions and not let them run away from you or ruin you. It means bridling your temper and not making excuses for immature emotional outbursts. This is a product of will more than skill. Everybody has power over their emotions if they are willing to tame them with the help of the Holy Spirit.

Communication skills

Communication can either destroy or strengthen any relationship. Intimacy and bonds are products of effective communication. Therefore, both the husband and the wife must understand how to express their intentions and feelings to each other in a way they'd fully understand. They must also know that males and females communicate differently.

Understanding common interests

Every marriage involves the union of two different people, but it should also share some distinct similarities, such as common interests, hobbies, faith, or similar political views. There needs to be a common meeting ground between the two.

Common background

Now, people from different backgrounds can have successful marriages, but these traits focus on increasing the likelihood of success. People with similar family backgrounds will find it easier to get along with each other because there'll be fewer things to adapt to.

A godly character is built through daily choices, embodying faithfulness and reliance on God's guidance.

STAGES OF MARRIAGE

1. THE LOVING RELATIONSHIP

In this initial stage, each partner finds joy in fulfilling the other's needs. There's an expectation that each partner's needs will be reciprocated, and marriage serves to solidify this sense of love and care. The couple is able to deepen their understanding of each other, irrespective of the distractions of daily life.

2. THE HONEYMOON IS OVER

At this stage, the dynamic shifts as one partner fails to meet the other's expectations, leading to disappointment and pain. The belief in mutual responsibility for each other's well-being persists, but behaviours become more manipulative, with attempts to please the partner aimed at restoring the initial state of "complete" love. Love and care are no longer unconditional, and partners oscillate between being critical and feeling hurt or disappointed when the relationship falls short of the ideal state.

3. GETTING EVEN

Disappointment and resentment transform into anger, leading to a power struggle marked by frequent retaliatory measures. The struggle serves as a defence mechanism against ongoing disappointment in the inability to reclaim the initial loving relationship. Arguments centre around control issues, such as money, sex, or time spent together. In extreme cases, extramarital affairs may occur as a means of hurting the spouse. The power struggle reflects a reaction to unmet expectations of unconditional love and acceptance, with couples attempting to control each other through power dynamics.

4. HANGING IN

Spouses, emotionally worn out and facing the threat of separation, divert their attention to other aspects of life rather than addressing existing conflicts. Despite the diminishing romantic love, the commitment to marriage remains, and the couple focuses on shared interests for the benefit of the family, such as building a house, raising children, or advancing their careers. While satisfaction in the relationship declines, a positive connection is established as the couple collaborates on joint enterprises.

5. DOING YOUR OWN THING

Spouses acknowledge the fantasy of expecting the other to fulfil their dependency needs. This realisation prompts increased independence and self-confidence as individuals seek gratification alone. The pursuit of happiness shifts from the spouse to external sources, marking a phase of reawakened passion but also a recognition of the limitations of the relationship.

6. GROWING UP

The final stage is characterised by an acceptance of reality, with a shift in focus to the present. Individuals in this stage develop self-reliance and recognise the necessity of maintaining a separate emotional identity for a mature relationship. Success in this stage involves accepting responsibility for one's pleasures and pains, as well as an increased availability to relate to others, especially one's mate, in a more complete way.

The most important takeaway from research on marital evolution is that all marriages and long-term partnerships have the potential to improve. Even when you feel like all hope is lost, remember that your relationship is constantly evolving and changing. Psychologists don't have all the answers, but we can say this for sure: how you feel about your marriage next year will be different from how you feel about it today.

Chapter Five

BUILDING A LASTING MARRIAGE (WITH DIVINE GUIDANCE)

HOME BUILDING

"Through wisdom a house is built, And by understanding it is established; By knowledge the rooms are filled With all precious and pleasant riches. A wise man is strong, Yes, a man of knowledge increases strength" (**PROVERBS 24:3-5; NKJV**).

"According to the grace of God which was given to me, as a wise master builder I have laid the foundation, and another builds on it. But let each one take heed how he builds on it. For no other foundation can anyone lay than that which is laid, which is Jesus Christ. Now if anyone builds on this foundation with gold, silver, precious stones, wood, hay, straw, each one's work will become clear; for the Day will declare it, because it will be revealed by fire; and the fire will test each one's work, of what sort it is" (**I CORINTHIANS 3:10-13; NKJV**).

TO BUILD MEANS

- Join together
- Form and set up
- Make further progress
- Become stronger
- Establish and strengthen

- Increase the capacity of something or somebody
- Create and construct
- Set up and assemble
- Make something in a particular way or pattern

Marriage is the most important decision a person can ever make.

More important than buying a car, a house, or starting a business.

Many people spend more money on their appearance, house, hobbies and cars than on their relationship.

Singer Robbie Williams spent millions of Pounds in one day to buy amazing super cars and got home, only to remember or discover he didn't have a driver's licence.

The government requires you to pass a test to get a licence to drive your car.

You need a building and content insurance certificate for your house.

But nobody conducts a test exam for anybody getting married.

Matter of fact, you get a marriage certificate at the beginning of your married journey on your wedding day without passing any test or sitting for any exams.

God gives you complete responsibility to choose your spouse. But always ready to lead, instruct, teach and direct.

"He who finds a wife finds a good thing, And obtains favor from the Lord" (**PROVERBS 18:22; NKJV**).

1. God gives you the Holy Spirit to direct you

2. Gives you a brain to think and have understanding

3. Gives you His word to regulate your decisions

4. Gives you pastors to counsel you

5. Gives you parents to train you

AFFECTION

Successful marriage is the application of knowledge (WISDOM).

"Wisdom is the principal thing; therefore get wisdom. And in all your getting, get understanding" (**PROVERBS 4:7; NKJV**).

Growing in understanding of the FOLLOWING enables couples to enjoy their marital relationship and last long, being able to help each other navigate the terrain of impeccable, purposeful, and resourceful marital destiny.

- Managing emotions
- Communication skills
- Anger management
- Cultivating affection
- Building intimacy
- Balancing and the need for date nights or days
- Money management with budgeting
- Consideration for one another
- Balancing your unified strengths
- Space management
- Dynamics of disagreements (disagree to agree)
- Handling in-laws so as not to become outlaws
- Love
- Deep affection management
- Tenderness
- Great attachment and interest in someone

Understanding makes love grow, flourish, blossom, and endure with excellent results.

- Love is not an emotion nor a feeling.
- Love is an intentional choice we make.
- Love is a force generated by decision.
- Genuine love has no feelings because feelings fade away.

- Love is an act of genuine personal will.
- Love is a debt you owe one another.
- Love is a commitment to meet the needs of one another for life.
- Love is caring (anticipating a need and meeting such a need without being asked).

"A new commandment I give to you, that you love one another; as I have loved you, that you also love one another" (**JOHN 13:34; NKJV**).

- The more valuable something is, the more you are willing to pay for it.
- The more valuable someone is, the more you care for them.

True love has no reason to it; there is no why.

If there is a reason for love, a condition will be attached to it, such as money, a good job, etc.

Where and when a condition exists, there will be expectations such as physical attributes, etc.

Where there are expectations, disappointment is guaranteed, such as body shape, etc.

Disappointment can lead to division in a relationship, such as betrayal or a broken trust.

Division leads to separation and divorce.

Divorce leads to death. Something dies in them.

Death creates dysfunctional families.

Dysfunctional families create social decay.

Social decay leads to rotten communities.

FINAL THOUGHTS

"When you make a vow to God, do not delay to pay it; For He has no pleasure in fools. Pay what you have vowed—Better not to vow than to vow and not pay. Do not let your mouth cause your flesh to sin, nor say before the messenger of God that it was an error. Why should God be angry at your excuse and destroy the work of your hands?" (**ECCLESIASTES 5:4-6; NKJV**).

'And I looked, and arose and said to the nobles, to the leaders, and to the rest of the people, "Do not be afraid of them. Remember the Lord, great and awesome, and fight for your brethren, your sons, your daughters, your wives, and your houses"' (**NEHEMIAH 4:14; NKJV**).

ATTRIBUTES OF MY HOME

(**ECCLESIASTES 4:9, 11-12; KJV**) *Two are better than one; because they have a good reward for their labour. Again, if two lie together, then they have heat: but how can one be warm alone? And if one prevail against him, two shall withstand him; and a threefold cord is not quickly broken.*

Through wisdom a house is built, And by understanding it is established; By knowledge the rooms are filled With all precious and pleasant riches (**PROVERBS 24:3-4; NKJV**).

Our house is not just a post code or postal address nor an architectural design, edifice or just a place to live in but a home built with Godly attributes and atmosphere. Our home gives support as a thriving dwelling place where memories and futures are created.

Let's examine the following attributes:

1. My home is a garden of LOVE (Loving God and Loving people).

Where love is created, enabled, breeds, multiplied and shared. We care for one another by showing love. Genuine love enables destiny to thrive, confidence building, peace and prosperity. Wholesome care is also festered.

Jesus said to him, "'You shall love the Lord your God with all your heart, with all your soul, and with all your mind.' This is the first and great commandment. And the second is like it: 'You shall love your neighbor as yourself' (**MATTHEW 22:37-39; NKJV**).

2. Place of REST and PEACE.

A recovery centre. Restoration station from all forms of storms, stress, wounds, negativities of life, etc. Wherever we ever go in the world, our home surely gives us emotional security, support and deliverance from all troubles, opposition, confusion and turmoil.

Because rest is a weapon, we're also equipped to face any situation in life. The home helps us to calm down and prepare for everyday battles of life.

I have found David my servant; with my holy oil have I anointed him: With whom my hand shall be established: mine arm also shall strengthen him. The enemy shall not exact upon him; nor the son of wickedness afflict him. And I will beat down his foes before his face, and plague them that hate him (**PSALM 89 VS 20-23**).

3. House of PRAYER and SPIRITUAL WARFARE (NOT a place of conflict and strife).

It's a place of spiritual warfare. Spiritually and mentally reinforcement is required to face life, adversaries and evil and wickedness of life. Spiritual battle axes are sharpened through spiritual warfare for ease of life, prosperity and fruitfulness of families. The home is not a wrestling ring nor a place of violence or place of physical abuse. When we're submitted to God through prayer and spiritual exercises, the Lord of host gets involved with us and in our cases, fights all our battles for us and gives us peace and victories. If the altar of prayer is abandoned in a home, God is edged out and a foothold is given to satan. Pray so you don't have to pray, because your life, family, destiny depends on it. Strategic intercession is ideal and compulsory in building and operating a robust godly home where fear of God reigns

Therefore submit to God. Resist the devil and he will flee from you (**JAMES 4:7**).

Finally, my brethren, be strong in the Lord and in the power of His might. 11 Put on the whole armor of God, that you may be able to stand against the wiles of the devil. For we do not wrestle against flesh and blood, but against principalities, against powers, against the rulers of the darkness of this age, against spiritual hosts of wickedness in the heavenly places (**EPHESIANS 6:10-12**).

4. A citadel of WISDOM and VISION, DREAMS and CREATIVITY.

Dreams and Vision and Creativity require a calm atmosphere to generate, germinate and flourish. Wisdom is profitable to do all things. Lack of wisdom creates chaos, disorder, death and confusion. A wise person increases in wisdom and a personality of understanding attains wise counsel. Lack of vision opens the door to unforced delays, errors, failure, when we don't know where we're going, everywhere looks like it. No more going round in circles. Get wisdom, get vision, receive dreams, creativity and idea hence comes with ease.

Where there is no revelation or vision, the people cast off restraint or are destroyed; But happy is he who keeps the law (**PROVERBS 29:18**).

5. My home has an enemy that wants to STEAL, KILL, & DESTROY.

The high time we know and recognise that satan is our enemy, the better equipped we shall be to receive life in Christ to the full till it overflows.

Your spouse is not the enemy neither are parents in-law. The real enemy is the devil. There's something looming and bigger behind every misbehaving, opposition, betrayal, wrongdoings, cause of pain, hurts, evildoing and brokenheartedness than the person seen with the physical eyes.

The thief does not come except to steal, and to kill, and to destroy. I have come that they may have life, and that they may have it more abundantly (**JOHN 10:10**).

Be sober, be vigilant; because your adversary the devil walks about like a roaring lion, seeking whom he may devour. [9] Resist him, steadfast in the faith, knowing that the same sufferings are experienced by your brotherhood in the world (**1 PETER 5:8-9**).

6. My home must have a Main Leader (The Man)—Protector, Provider, Promoter, and Encourager.

God made man in His image and after His likeness fully resourced to operate in every capacity allotted and called to live. Man leaves his father and mother to cleave to his wife and be one with her. Everything rises and falls on the man, he's the foundation that's built on. A foundation must have capacity and shock absorbers to withstand terror, earthquake, cracks and breakdown. Must be able to carry everything to be built on it. Husbands must love their wives as Christ loves the church. Fathers must fight for their families and enjoy the partnership of their wives in training their children in the way of the Lord and building deliberately and intentionally, a home God can be proud of.

Seeing that Abraham shall surely become a great and mighty nation, and all the nations of the earth shall be blessed in him? For I know him, that he will command his children and his household after him, and they shall keep the way of the Lord, to do justice and judgment; that the Lord may bring upon Abraham that which he hath spoken of him (**GENESIS 18:18-19**).

Leaders have enough energy for OTHER PEOPLE.

KILLERS OF MARRIAGE

If care is not taken, years and seasons of solid building of marriages can come crashing down in a blink of an eye. Keeping our eyes on the driving seat to attain a glorious future cannot be over emphasised. Winners don't quit, quitters don't win. Whosoever began a good work is faithful to complete it with determination and without fear or contradictions. Keep building, keep believing for the best, greater and better days are ahead of you.

CHECK OUT THE FOLLOWING KILLERS:

1. Laziness kills marriage.

2. Suspicion kills marriage.

3. Lack of trust kills marriage.

4. Lack of mutual respect kills marriage.

5. Unforgiveness, bitterness, hatred, malice, and anger kill marriage.

6. Unnecessary arguments kill marriage.

7. Keeping secrets from your spouse kills marriage.

8. Infidelity (financial, emotional, psychological, material, etc.) kills marriage.

9. Poor communication kills marriage.

10. Lies can easily kill a marriage; be sincere with your spouse in every aspect.

11. Prioritising parents/family over your spouse kills a marriage.

12. Lack of or unenjoyable intimacy can kill a marriage.

13. Nagging kills marriage.

14. Too much talk and careless words kill a marriage.

15. Spending little time with your spouse can kill your marriage.

16. Being too independent-minded kills marriage.

17. Love for partying, material possessions, impulse buying, and financial indiscipline can kill a marriage.

18. Exposing your spouse's inadequacies to your parents or siblings kills marriage.

19. Neglecting spiritual practices and not praying together kills not only marriage but also your life.

20. Spurning correction and reprimand kills marriage.

21. Always wearing a sad face and being moody kills a marriage.

22. Extreme feminism advocacy kills marriage.

23. Male chauvinism kills marriage.

24. Uncontrolled temper and anger kill a marriage.

25. Not understanding your role and responsibility in marriage as instituted by God kills marriage.

26. Ignoring the spiritual, emotional, and physical needs of your spouse can kill a marriage.

27. Threatening the security of a spouse will have detrimental effects on the marriage.

28. Lack of knowledge of and obedience to the Word of God kills marriage.

EMOTIONALLY HEALTHY MARRIAGE

Marriages are made in Heaven but maintained on earth and guess what, it's hard work, not for the faint hearted. You don't have to be perfect to be married but must be ready for change, ready to change, being changed, growing up and evolving which requires being involved and being present all the way.

Marriage also serves as a catalyst to enable you to fulfill God's plan for your life. Marry well, marry right.

Learn, research and understand your spouse to enable you to be in right frame of mind. Your spouse can be your best friend forever. You can create together for life all forms of memories, healthy life, excitement, momentums, thrillers. You can take the world together. Flourishing and growing together.

Thriving together in any environment.

18 And the LORD God said, It is not good that the man should be alone; I will make him an help meet for him.

21 And the LORD God caused a deep sleep to fall upon Adam, and he slept: and he took one of his ribs, and closed up the flesh instead thereof;

22 and the rib, which the LORD God had taken from man, made he a woman, and brought her unto the man.

23 And Adam said, This is now bone of my bones, and flesh of my flesh: she shall be called Woman, because she was taken out of Man.

24 Therefore shall a man leave his father and his mother, and shall cleave unto his wife: and they shall be one flesh.

25 And they were both naked, the man and his wife, and were not ashamed (**GENESIS 2:18, 21-25; KJV**).

Jesus is the chief maintenance officer of marriages.

I am the vine, ye are the branches: He that abideth in me, and I in him, the same bringeth forth much fruit: for without me ye can do nothing (**JOHN 15:5; KJV**).

And therefore will the LORD wait, that he may be gracious unto you, and therefore will he be exalted, that he may have mercy upon you: for the LORD is a God of judgment: blessed are all they that wait for him (**ISAIAH 30:18; KJV**).

The LORD is good unto them that wait for him, To the soul that seeketh him (**LAMENTATIONS 3:25; KJV**).

Ye that fear the LORD, trust in the LORD: He is their help and their shield (**PSALM 115:11; KJV**).

And they that know thy name will put their trust in thee: For thou, LORD, hast not forsaken them that seek thee (**PSALM 9:10; KJV**).

Let them shout for joy, and be glad, that favour my righteous cause: Yea, let them say continually, Let the LORD be magnified, which hath pleasure in the prosperity of his servant (**PSALM 35:27; KJV**).

If you wait for the perfect wife or the perfect husband, it isn't going to just happen. Let me tell you why: we're all broken. That's okay because God still loves you. However, you need to understand that anyone you marry will be broken.

Everybody is broken, but some people are a lot more broken than others. And you need to avoid them, no matter how good-looking, rich, or nice they are. You need to assess the emotional health of your potential partner before entering a long-term relationship.

Study after study has shown that 80 percent of all separations and divorces happen because one or both of the partners are emotionally unhealthy.

CHECKLIST OF EMOTIONAL HEALTH FACTORS

This is what God says you need to avoid.

1. Whoever you marry must not be nursing any uncontrolled anger.

PROVERBS 22:24 (NIV) says, *"Do not make friends with a hot-tempered person; do not associate with one easily angered".*

Do you know why? Because uncontrolled anger reveals deep insecurity and low self-worth.

2. Whoever you marry must not be stuck in an addiction.

PROVERBS 23:20 (TEV) says, *"Don't associate with people who drink too much wine or stuff themselves with food".*

Only two things are mentioned here, food and alcohol, but there are a thousand ways to get addicted.

3. Whoever you marry must not be harbouring bitterness.

Bitterness is like a poison—it eats you alive. Whatever you resent, you begin to resemble. To stop resenting, you've got to release it.

HEBREWS 12:15 (GNT), *"Guard against turning back from the grace of God. Let no one become like a bitter plant that grows up and causes many troubles with its poison".*

4. Whoever you marry must not be selfish. Why?

PROVERBS 28:25 says, *"Selfishness only causes trouble."*

When it comes down to it, the number one cause of conflict in marriage is simple: selfishness.

5. Whoever you marry must not be greedy.

PROVERBS 15:27 (NLT)

"Greed brings grief to the whole family".

If you marry a greedy spouse, you will be in debt for your entire life.

6. Whoever you marry must be generous and kind.

"A generous man will prosper; he who refreshes others will himself be refreshed" (**PROVERBS 11:25; NIV**).

And, *"Those who are kind benefit themselves, but the cruel bring ruin on themselves"* (**PROVERBS 11:17**).

7. Whoever you marry must tell the truth.

PROVERBS 20:7 (GWT) *"A righteous person lives on the basis of his integrity. Blessed are his children after he is gone".*

Love is based on trust, and trust is based on truth. If you don't tell me the truth, I can't trust you. And if I can't trust you, how can I love you?

You might be thinking, "I'm not sure if I'll ever find anybody who fits this." Oh, really? I did. And you can, too.

Chapter Six

MAKING MARRIAGE WORK OUT

You can have heaven on earth in your marriage, and that depends on your thinking and belief system. Making grass greener requires concerted efforts and smart, hard work.

STEPS TO MARRIAGE WORKOUT

"God always gives His best to those who leave the choice to Him."

1. There is nothing that threatens the security of a man more than the thought of another man competing for the attention and affection of his wife. Nothing is more painful. Nothing is more disrespectful. Nothing is more insulting. Nothing is more belittling and degrading.

2. Marriage flourishes when the couple work together as a team, when both husband and wife decide that winning together is more important than keeping score.

Good marriages don't just happen. They are a product of hard work.

HOMEWORK: DO A THOROUGH STUDY OF PSALM 133.

3. Your children are watching you and forming lasting opinions on love, commitment, and marriage based on what they see in you. Give them hope. Make them look forward to marriage.

I rejoiced greatly that I have found some of your children walking in truth, as we received commandment from the Father (**2 JOHN 1:4**).

4. Husbands: The reason other women look attractive is that someone is taking good care of them. Grass is always green where it is watered. Instead of drooling over the green grass on the other side of the fence, work on yours and water it regularly. Any man can admire a beautiful woman, but it takes a true gentleman to make a woman admirable and beautiful.

Then the Lord God took the man and put him in the garden of Eden to tend and keep it (**GENESIS 2:15**).

5. When a husband puts his wife first above everyone and everything except God, it gives his wife the sense of security and honour that every wife hungers for.

Let nothing be done through selfish ambition or conceit, but in lowliness of mind let each esteem others better than himself (**PHILIPPIANS 2:3**).

6. A successful marriage doesn't require a big house, a perfect spouse, lots of money, or an expensive car. There is nothing bad with any of these, though. You can have all the above and still have a miserable marriage. A successful marriage requires honesty, undying commitment, selfless love, and Jesus at the centre of it all.

Let love be without hypocrisy. Abhor what is evil. Cling to what is good.

Be kindly affectionate to one another with brotherly love, in honor giving preference to one another (**ROMANS 12:9-10**).

7. Pray for your spouse every day, in the morning, afternoon, and evening. Don't wait until there is a problem. Don't wait until there is an affair. Don't wait until something bad happens. Don't wait until your spouse is tempted. Shield your spouse with prayer and cover your marriage with the fence of prayer.

Be sober, be vigilant; because your adversary the devil walks about like a roaring lion, seeking whom he may devour (**1 PETER 5:8**).

8. The people you surround yourself with have a lot of influence on your marriage. Friends can build or break your marriage; choose them wisely.

A man who has friends must himself be friendly, But there is a friend who sticks closer than a brother (**PROVERBS 18:24**).

9. One spouse cannot build a marriage alone when the other spouse is committed to destroying it. Marriage works when both husband and wife work together as a team to build their marriage.

Can two walk together, unless they are agreed? (**AMOS 3:3**).

10. Don't take your spouse for granted. Don't take advantage of your spouse's meekness and goodness. Don't mistake your spouse's loyalty for desperation. Don't misuse or abuse your spouse's trust. You may end up regretting losing someone who meant so much to you and you mean so much to.

Submitting to one another in the fear of God (**EPHESIANS 5:21**).

11. Beware of marital advice from single people. Regardless of how sincere their advice may be, most of it is theoretical and lacks real-life experience. If you really need godly advice, seek it from God-fearing, impartial and prayerful mature couples whose resolve has been tested by time and shaped by trials.

He who walks with wise men will be wise, But the companion of fools will be destroyed (**PROVERBS 13:20**).

12. Dear wife, dear husband, don't underestimate the power of the tongue in your marriage. The tongue has the power to crush your marriage or build it up. Don't let the devil use your tongue to kill your spouse's image, joy, self-confidence, peace and aspirations. Let God use your tongue to build up your marriage and bless and praise your spouse.

The wise woman builds her house, But the foolish pulls it down with her hands (**PROVERBS 14:1**).

MAKING MARRIAGE HEALTHY

Emphasis on study and absolute meditation of Ephesians 5:21-33.

'To make healthy' means to be strong, full of life, prosperous, and sound. It means being fresh and robust, to be flourishing, fruitful, sickness free, thriving.

To make marriage healthy, let's look at the following operations:

- Island of Self {Focus on good things, good sides, attributes about your spouse}.

- Major more on the positive. If you and your spouse focus on each other's faults, you will destroy your marriage. No one is perfect, but you can accept the imperfections in your spouse.

- *"Love covers all sins" (Proverbs 10:12) and "keeps no record of wrongs"* (1 Corinthians 13:5; NIV).

- When you focus on the good things about your spouse, the not-so-good things fade away with time.

- God's Design (Your spouse is God's best for you)

- Talk up your spouse; be their biggest fan. Brag about them.

- Wives, it's so meaningful when you tell your husband that you believe in him and in his ability to do the right thing and vice versa from the husband.

- Husbands, I've found that you can never tell your wife, "I love you", often enough. In fact, there's magic in those three little words, so make sure both of you say them to each other every day. Be sincere in what you say, but also make sure you say positive things out loud to each other when you think of them. It's a game changer.

TWO AS ONE (RECOGNISE THE POWER OF CLEAVING TOGETHER)

There are a thousand different ways to express love to one another and surprise your spouse. A phone call in the middle of the day. An unexpected gift. His favourite dessert. Her favourite perfume. Being primped when he comes home. Telling her how great she looks. Doing something fun together that you really enjoy, like having a movie night with popcorn or taking a drive through the country. The Bible encourages us not to despise "the day of small things" (Zechariah 4:10). Learn what puts the sparkle in your spouse's eye and do it. Remember: when spouses in a marriage play together they undoubtedly stay together.

HONEYMOON ENDS

The happiest marriage is the union of two forgiven forgivers. When you know how much God has forgiven you, you can then extend forgiveness to your spouse on a regular basis. Otherwise, anger and unforgiveness will burn a hole in your heart and eventually explode in some unexpected ways. So, learn to let it go. Practise saying, "I'm sorry."

And *"do not let the sun go down while you are still angry"* (**EPHESIANS 4:26; NIV**).

HANDLING DIFFERENCES

Talk things out. If the three rules of real estate are location, location, and location, then the three most important traits for a successful marriage are communication, communication, and communication. Learn early on to be honest and open with each other, *"Speaking the truth in love"* (**EPHESIANS 4:15**).

HARDEST WORD

Broker your responses to your spouse wisely. Husbands, trade neglect for attention. Focus on your wife. Find out what she needs and when she needs it, and give her your undivided attention. Turn your thoughts toward her thoughts and her feelings, and work on expressing your own. Wives, trade nagging for grace. Ask yourself, "Can I say it kindly? Can I relay the message so that he can hear the grace in my intent?" And remember: timing is part of grace. Love him enough to let him be wrong and give him grace when he is. Also vice versa, the man needs to also give grace to his wife.

Providing a strong, sheltering love for your wife takes time and energy, but it's worth it. Consistently loving her well will stabilise your relationship, allowing God to work in the two of you to build the oneness He wants in your marriage.

STRONG SHELTER

Time is of the essence, so make the most of your time with your spouse. It's more valuable than getting that promotion, making another buck, or hanging out with your buddies.

Learn the value of time. Don't waste it.

There is *"a time to love"* (**ECCLESIASTES 3:8**).

HOMEMAKER

Don't forget to thank your spouse for the little things. Did your husband mow the lawn? Did your wife sew a button on your shirt? Be grateful. And when your spouse expresses appreciation, respond warmly.

"Let the peace of God rule in your hearts, to which also you were called in one body; and be thankful" (**COLOSSIANS 3:15**).

THE LOVE AFFAIR

Keep the romance alive. Flirt with your spouse. Make yourselves attractive and appealing to each other in dress and actions.

"My beloved is mine, and I am his" (**SONG OF SOLOMON 2:16**).

The way you courted your spouse is the same way you keep them. Keep chasing, pursuit is the proof of desire.

BUILDING HOME

Hands are for holding and folding. It's been said that the couple that prays together stays together. So, take everything to God in prayer, and remember to always thank Him for His goodness.

"Whoever offers praise glorifies Me" (**PSALM 50:23**).

Praise keeps the sunshine in your soul and God's smile on your marriage.

Chapter Seven

MARITAL TRANSFORMATION

And do not be conformed to this world, but be transformed by the renewing of your mind, that you may prove what is that good and acceptable and perfect will of God (**ROMANS 12:2**).

And the Lord God said, "It is not good that man should be alone; I will make him a helper comparable to him" (**GENESIS 2:18; NKJV**).

Now the Lord God said, It is not good (sufficient, satisfactory) that the man should be alone; I will make him a helper meet (suitable, adapted, complementary) for him (**AMPC**).

Marriage is a ministry which involves managing and ministering to one another.

Marriage is about studying, knowing, and understanding the weaknesses of your spouse and helping them recover and become better people.

Marriage is about seeing your spouse fall down and helping them get back up and achieve stability, strength, efficiency, success, and a balanced life.

The major things on a man's mind are never discussed in church. We talk about all other things but these:

POWER, MONEY, AND SEX

Single people of marriageable age are waiting for a marriage partner.

God wants everyone to be married, except those called Eunuchs, who are set apart for God's special assignments.

Then God blessed them, and God said to them, "Be fruitful and multiply; fill the earth and subdue it; have dominion over the fish of the sea, over the birds of the air, and over every living thing that moves on the earth" (**GENESIS 1:28**).

Singles must look forward, waiting in anticipation, in hope, expectantly, and in joy.

PREPARATION IN WAITING

And let us not grow weary while doing good, for in due season we shall reap if we do not lose heart (**GALATIANS 6:9**).

Then Naomi, her mother-in-law: said to her, "My daughter, shall I not seek security for you, that it may be well with you." Now Boaz, whose young women you were with, is he not our relative? In fact, he is winnowing barley tonight at the threshing floor. Therefore wash yourself and anoint yourself, put on your best garment and go down to the threshing floor; but do not make yourself known to the man until he has finished eating and drinking. Then it shall be, when he lies down, that you shall notice the place where he lies; and you shall go in, uncover his feet, and lie down; and he will tell you what you should do." And she said to her, "All that you say to me I will do" (**RUTH 3:1-5**).

- Serve somebody, group of people, your organisation, your environment, and community. Do what you can to help others. Receive mentorship.

- Wash up, clean up, tidy up, renew, and refresh. Develop yourself and act for the future.

- Anoint & perfume yourself like the person you want to smell like.

- Change your garment & dress up for the future you desire & look forward to.

- Don't hide in darkness, loneliness, or pity. Get away from harmful people.

Blessed is the man Who walks not in the counsel of the ungodly, Nor stands in the path of sinners, Nor sits in the seat of the scornful (**PSALM 1:1**).

- Follow instructions prayerfully

Wherefore lay apart all filthiness and superfluity of naughtiness, and receive with meekness the engrafted word, which is able to save your souls (**JAMES 1:21**).

MARRIAGE IS HONOURABLE

Most wives are prayerful, and they can adapt and transform to bring the best to their family.

Marriage is honorable among all, and the bed undefiled; but fornicators and adulterers God will judge (**HEBREWS 13:4**).

Don't marry because:

- You want to keep yourself from sinning,
- Your mates are getting married
- You are in love
- Time is going

But rather MARRY because you know and have a good understanding of the person you want to spend the rest of your life with. We never stop learning from studying and getting to know our spouses.

Your marriage plays a big role in your motivation, joy, and sense of uniqueness and destiny fulfilment. Your best comes out.

Therefore I desire that the younger widows marry, bear children, manage the house, give no opportunity to the adversary to speak reproachfully (**1 TIMOTHY 5:14**).

He who finds a wife finds a good thing, And obtains favor from the Lord (**PROVERBS 18:22**).

Houses and riches are an inheritance from fathers, But a prudent wife is from the Lord (**PROVERBS 19:14**).

Wives, submit yourselves unto your own husbands, as it is fit in the Lord. Husbands, love your wives, and be not bitter against them (**COLOSSIANS 3:18-19**).

Security and significance are needed by both men and women, regardless of their circumstances.

Husbands, love your wives, even as Christ also loved the church, and gave himself for it; that he might sanctify and cleanse it with the washing of water by the word, that he might present it to himself a glorious church, not having spot, or wrinkle, or any such thing; but that it should be holy and without blemish. So ought men to love their wives as their own bodies. He that loveth his wife loveth himself (**EPHESIANS 5:25-28**).

Provision: Food, shelter.

Protection: Preservation, shield.

Promotion: Encouragement, boosting confidence, and worth. Helping with dreams & visions of their life.

DEVIL'S TRAPS IN YOUR HOMES

Be sober, be vigilant; because your adversary the devil walks about like a roaring lion, seeking whom he may devour (**1 PETER 5:8**).

The devil knows that when husband & wife have lost control spiritually, the children will be easy meat.

As long as they remain spiritually strong, the children remain under the strong spiritual cover of God's grace.

1. WIFE OR HUSBAND – BEATING (PHYSICAL ABUSE)

A Christian brother should know that no matter what the problem may be with the woman, there is always a better way to deal with it than resorting to beating his wife. It should never be done!

"Husbands, likewise, dwell with them with understanding, giving honor to the wife, as to the weaker vessel, and as being heirs together of the grace of life, that your prayers may not be hindered" (**1 PETER 3:7**).

Needless to say, this is a scripture every married Christian man should hold close to his heart if indeed he wants the will of God to be done in his family.

2. WITHHOLDING SEX (EMOTIONAL ABUSE)

For the married couple, especially the women, one thing (among others) that they must essentially consider a spiritual taboo is the tendency to use sex as a weapon by withholding it from their husbands as a form of punishment, manipulation, or control.

This appears to be quite common with married women, but a true and wise Christian woman will know that indulging in such practice is a trap of the devil. There is always a better way to deal with marital issues than resorting to committing this error, which, apart from the potential hazardous consequences, cannot be justified scripturally.

"Do not deprive one another except with consent for a time, that you may give yourselves to fasting and prayer; and come together again so that Satan does not tempt you because of your lack of self-control" (**1 CORINTHIANS 7:5**).

3. ADULTERY

(Wounds, blows, strife, bitterness, revenge, selfishness)

Defiling the matrimonial bed is an error which most people will easily talk about in marriage. It is not only a spiritual error but also an act that is morally condemnable. It does not require much belabouring in this discourse, since it has been clearly discussed in the Bible.

"Marriage is honorable among all, and the bed undefiled; but fornicators and adulterers God will judge" (**HEBREWS 13:4**).

"Little foxes" give rise to bigger issues (including adultery) after they have existed for a long time in that relationship.

For why should you, my son, be enraptured by an immoral woman, And be embraced in the arms of a seductress? (**PROVERBS 5:20; NKJV**)

Any form of dissatisfaction, on either side of a marital relationship, must be promptly dealt with and never taken for granted.

NEED FOR TRANSFORMATION

1. Admit you're in trouble in your marriage.

See the signs and face it:

- When you stopped talking.
- When you don't want to go home and always want to confide in other people.

"Therefore what God has joined together, let not man separate" (Mark 10:9; NKJV).

2. Confirm your spiritual differences

Assess the spiritual maturity of your spouse regularly. (Grow in the Word, hunger for God, knowledge of the Word, and know God).

For how do you know, O wife, whether you will save your husband? Or how do you know, O husband, whether you will save your wife? (**I CORINTHIANS 7:16**).

But also for this very reason, giving all diligence, add to your faith virtue, to virtue knowledge, (**2 PETER 1:5**).

3. Discover and recognise any crack

Third party or voice messing with your environment. Evaluate earlier influences in life—parents, friends, teachers, colleagues, etc. Check out any 3rd voice speaking to your spouse (In-laws, sicknesses and diseases, devils, sympathisers).

And besides they learn to be idle, wandering about from house to house, and not only idle but also gossips and busybodies, saying things which they ought not (**I TIMOTHY 5:13**).

4. Acknowledge the difference in one another.

Identify and meet the needs of your spouse (e.g., sports, recreation, early or late riser).

- Acknowledge the good and compliment your spouse.
- Invest energy, labour, time, and what matters to your spouse.
- Observe mood swings in your woman because of the menstrual cycle or menopause and dwell according to knowledge.

5. Seek qualified counselling.

Seek guidance and counselling from godly, competent, respected persons if needed. Not from people who mock you and gossip about your faults and shortcomings.

Where there is no counsel, the people fall; But in the multitude of counselors there is safety (**PROVERBS 11:4**).

Listen to counsel and receive instruction, That you may be wise in your latter days (**PROVERBS 19:20**).

6. Make time to honour your spouse.

- (Honour removes stress, doesn't shame or belittle spouse, trusting, and never tear down or cut you apart).
- Create memories in your relationship.
- Dwell with her according to knowledge.
- Create pleasures for you and your spouse.

Be kindly affectionate to one another with brotherly love, in honor giving preference to one another (**ROMANS 12:10**).

7. Dialogue.

Conversations seasoned with salt.

Dialogue matters in a marriage.

Listen and create conversation with your spouse. Talk, talk, and keep talking.

Let your speech always be with grace, seasoned with salt, that you may know how you ought to answer each one (**COLOSSIANS 4:6**).

RELATIONSHIP MANAGEMENT

PERSONALITY TRAITS

Therefore, putting away lying, "Let each one of you speak truth with his neighbor," for we are members of one another. "Be angry, and do not sin": do not let the sun go down on your wrath, nor give place to the devil. Let him who stole steal no longer, but rather let him labor, working with his hands what is good, that he may have something to give him who has need. Let no corrupt word proceed out of your mouth, but what is good for necessary edification, that it may impart grace to the hearers. And do not grieve the Holy Spirit of God, by whom you were sealed for the day of redemption. Let all bitterness, wrath, anger, clamor, and evil speaking be put away from you, with all malice. And be kind to one another, tenderhearted, forgiving one another, even as God in Christ forgave you (**EPHESIANS 4:25-32; NKJV**).

Two are better than one, Because they have a good reward for their labor. For if they fall, one will lift up his companion. But woe to him who is alone when he falls, For he has no one to help him up. Again, if two lie down together, they will keep warm; But how can one be warm alone? Though one may be overpowered by another, two can withstand him. And a threefold cord is not quickly broken (**ECCLESIASTES 4:9-12**).

1. Super-Spiritual Personality Trait

Description:

- Person that escapes reality and hides behind the convenience of spirituality.
- Speaks in scattered, disconnected spiritual phrases to avoid confrontation.

Personal Adjustments:

- Remind yourself that natural order is first.
- Listen more (slow to speak, swift to hear).
- Handle your situations with spiritual wisdom.

Relationship Handling:

- Don't get into spiritual debates or scripture quoting with them.
- Resolve every situation on time with such persons.

2. Passive (Irresponsible) Personality Trait

Description:

- Person who has others taking care of them.
- Avoids decision-making; prefers others to decide and make up their mind for them.
- Lives an easy-going life with others making few demands on them.

Personal Adjustments:

- Have close allies hold you accountable—a little personal reporting system.

- When you process your emotions, do not think someone is controlling you.

Relationship Handling:

- Leave room for them to make personal decisions.
- Pick your words carefully due to your better understanding.
- Give them the benefit of the doubt.

3. Super-Sensitive Personality Trait

Description:

- Easily offended.
- Jumps to conclusions without proof.
- Quickly suspects others of unfair treatment without significant proof.

Personal Adjustments:

- Always check the first thoughts that come to your mind.
- Give others the benefit of the doubt for their behavior (second chance).

Relationship Handling:

- Compliment them often.
- Help them focus on facts.
- Be apologetic.

4. Socially Abusive Personality Trait

Description:

- Person who has inferiority and insecurity borne out of past deprivation.
- Handles life and situations with rudeness.
- Intimidates others through rudeness and harassment.

Personal Adjustments:

- Know who you are in Christ.
- Depend on the Holy Spirit to restrain your flesh.

Relationship Handling:

- Never challenge them in public.
- Speak softly during conflict.
- Define and lay good grounds for respect—and enforce it.

5. Complaining, Depressing Personality Trait

Description:

- Tends to magnify and intensify negative situations.
- Justifies their victim status.
- Justifies their right to be unhappy.
- Expects pity from others.

Personal Adjustments:

- Don't get frustrated with yourself.
- Affirm positive things out loud.
- Stay under the blood of Jesus constantly.

Relationship Handling:

- Compliment them regularly.
- Encourage them as winners.
- Never give a listening ear to their exaggerations.

6. Seductive, Manipulating Personality Trait

Description:

- Person brought up to hustle in life.
- Has difficulty forming true, lasting relationships.
- Struggles with genuine connection and trust.

Personal Adjustments:

- Show yourself more friendly.
- Open up fresh conversations with others.
- Take life one day at a time.
- Believe in others.
- Give people second chances.

Relationship Handling:

- Set relationship boundaries and don't be carried away.
- Enjoy their friendship without being suspicious.
- Encourage them to invest more in friendships.

7. Controlling, Perfectionist Trait

Description:

- Their passion for excellence makes life unbearable for others.
- Expects everyone to act and think like them.
- Blinded by imperfection in others.
- Focuses on flaws instead of appreciating progress.
- Has a superiority complex.

Personal Adjustments:

- Curb your zeal to make others think and be like you.
- Respect others' developmental stages.
- Help others by teaching them to be their best.

Relationship Handling:

- Don't be frustrated with them.
- Take full responsibility—it helps to calm them.
- Ask them for solutions.

8. Acceptance-Needy Personality Trait

Description:

- Aggressively needs acceptance due to a poor self-image.

- Suppresses feelings instead of expressing them.
- Forfeits their right to be accepted.
- Undervalues themselves.

Personal Adjustments:

- Strengthen your relationship with Jesus Christ.
- Build your self-esteem.
- Believe in yourself.
- Refuse to be abused by others.
- Humble yourself before God for transformation.

Relationship Handling:

- Humble yourself with them.
- Help them express their feelings.
- Applaud their initiatives.
- Appreciate their emotions.
- Deliberately detach from their acceptance-needy culture.

Chapter Eight

TOXIC RELATIONSHIP

Do you find yourself in a toxic relationship and think that you might be the cause?

Toxic relationships are unhealthy relationships that cause ongoing emotional pain for those involved.

Toxic relationships are embedded with negativity, abuse, and belittling others and are very complex.

ECCLESIASTES 10:1 KJV – *Dead flies cause the ointment of the apothecary to send forth a stinking savour: so doth a little folly him that is in reputation for wisdom and honour.*

1 CORINTHIANS 15:33 KJV – *Be not deceived: evil communications corrupt good manners.*

SONG OF SOLOMON 2:15 KJV – *Take us the foxes, The little foxes, That spoil the vines: For our vines have tender grapes.*

"As iron sharpens iron, So a man sharpens the countenance of his friend" (**PROVERBS 27:17**).

Toxic defined:

1. Someone or something destructive

2. An asset with no value

3. To be harmful or deadly

4. Have unpleasant feelings

5. Something or someone that can injure or affect negatively, causing injury

6. Ability to cause offence

As human beings, we are made for connection, cooperation, collaboration, and community. Being in a relationship is essential for all areas of our lives and is part of God's original plan. Whether in ministry, family, business, or day-to-day operations, we are open to skills, gifts, resources, and talents we don't possess. This becomes a vehicle for our learning and impacting others.

This is a prayer to God to give us the grace to maintain healthy, essential relationships and eliminate toxic ones. A new you must emerge to appreciate, enrich, adapt, and get the best out of communities.

Not everyone pushes us to be better. Some people stop us from following our dreams or talk us out of taking a risk, and we don't always realise that it's happening. So, it's important to be aware and consciously choose who we spend time with to limit spending time with toxic people.

TOXIC PERSONALITIES

1. THE COMPLAINERS

"These are grumblers, complainers, walking according to their own lusts; and they mouth great swelling words, flattering people to gain advantage" (JUDE 1:16).

Complainers are people who are always complaining about how bad their life, job, marriage, or whatever is. They constantly whine about everything but never take action.

Being around a complainer can take a toll on you—maybe you begin to join in on the complaints, and before you know it, you adopt their same way of negative thinking. That pessimism is contagious, which is why you should think twice before sitting down with a complainer.

2. THE ENTITLED

(Believe oneself to be inherently deserving of privileges or special treatment and think the world will revolve around them).

"A faithful man will abound with blessings, But he who hastens to be rich will not go unpunished" (**PROV. 28:20**).

These are the people who feel entitled to certain things in life, as if they do not have to work for anything, and believe that those around them owe them something. They are also the ones who will try to talk you out of following your dreams. They love freebies too much.

This mindset can be detrimental to a person trying to be successful. It blocks your determination and can kill your motivation in a heartbeat. Know this: You, or anyone else, are not entitled to anything. If you want the good life, you have to create it.

3. THE CONFORMERS

"For the turning away of the simple will slay them, And the complacency of fools will destroy them;" (**PROVERBS 1:32; NKJV**).

"O you simple ones, understand prudence, And you fools, be of an understanding heart" (**PROVERBS 8:5; NKJV**).

Conformers are the most popular of all. They are the ones who conform to the limits set on them. They do not have any dreams they are chasing after, and they are not doing something that goes against the status quo. They never go the extra mile. Just the usual, normal life. Nothing extraordinary, very average and mediocre in nature. They are simply living like robots—waking up, working 40 hours a week at a job they hate, going home, sleeping, and repeating the cycle all over again.

SHARK IN AN AQUARIUM

There are many people who are content with this, and that is perfectly fine.

4. THE PARTY ANIMALS

"envy, murders, drunkenness, revelries, and the like; of which I tell you beforehand, just as I also told you in time past, that those who practice such

things will not inherit the kingdom of God" (**GALATIANS 5:21**).

The party animal might be fun, but beware—they can distract you from your dreams.

Don't get me wrong; you should take time to relax and clear your head on occasion. By making partying a priority, you're distracting yourself and breaking focus on your goals. In order to grow as a person, you have to grow up first.

5. THE DOUBTERS.

"And He said to them, "Why are you troubled? And why do doubts arise in your hearts?" (**LUKE 24:38; NKJV**).

"And immediately Jesus stretched out His hand and caught him, and said to him, "O you of little faith, why did you doubt?"" (**MATTHEW 14:31; NKJV**).

Doubters can be downers—they will listen to your big dreams, but they will be the first ones to tell you they don't think it is a good idea or not to get your hopes up. They are the ones who believe you have to "be somebody" in order to do something extravagant.

Therefore, identify the doubters in your group, surround yourself with supportive people, and know those who encourage you and lift your spirits when you are losing motivation.

TOXIC ATTITUDES

When we invite Jesus into our hearts, He moves in—and He does not timidly co-exist with our sin. He is a ruthless warrior, and He goes on a loving rampage until every area of our rebellious hearts has been conquered. He slays our pride, kills our greed, and shows no mercy for any sinful behaviour that has controlled us. Your choice is to cooperate with this process or to drag it out longer than necessary because you don't want Him to meddle with your private life.

Below are five attitudes God wants to change in all of us. Bad attitudes can keep us out of our promised land. They can hinder God's work in our lives. They can quench the Holy Spirit. If you have not yielded these attitudes to Him, let the Holy Spirit move in today and begin the process of demolition.

1. STUBBORNNESS

Dogged determination not to change one's attitude or position on something

For rebellion is as the sin of witchcraft, And stubbornness is as iniquity and idolatry. Because you have rejected the word of the LORD, He also has rejected you from being king'" (**1 SAMUEL 15:23**).

Is your daily prayer: "Not my will, but Yours be done"? God wants surrender. Don't be a stubborn foot-dragger or a Jonah who runs when God calls you.

2. NEGATIVITY

'To console those who mourn in Zion, To give them beauty for ashes, The oil of joy for mourning, The garment of praise for the spirit of heaviness; That they may be called trees of righteousness, The planting of the LORD, that He may be glorified'" (**ISAIAH 61:3**).

Pessimism, criticalness, cynicism, darkness.

Joy is a fruit of the Holy Spirit, but you would never know this when you are around certain Christians. They never learnt to rejoice in the hard times. They always expect the worst. Their faith is extinguished by fear and doubt. Let God exchange all doom and gloom for a garment of praise.

3. SELF-CENTREDNESS

"Let each of you look out not only for his own interests, but also for the interests of others (**PHILIPPIANS 2:4**).

For all seek their own, not the things which are of Christ Jesus (**PHILIPPIANS 2:21**).

The essence of sin is selfishness, but as the church, we learn to love and serve one another and esteem each other higher than ourselves. Learn to put others first.

4. WOUNDEDNESS

"For I am poor and needy, And my heart is wounded within me" (**PSALM 109:22**).

"But He was wounded for our transgressions, He was bruised for our iniquities; The chastisement for our peace was upon Him, And by His stripes we are healed" (**ISAIAH 53:5**).

Hurting people hurts others. We've all been hurt at some point in our lives. God calls us to forgive and heal up, no matter how much pain we endured when we were betrayed, disrespected, violated, or overlooked. God wants to wipe away your tears, but He can't heal you if you harbour hatred towards the people who hurt you. Forgiveness is a choice, not a feeling. Love anyway.

5. FAULT-FINDING

PHILIPPIANS 2:14 commands us:

"Do all things without complaining and disputing".

Many people are finger-pointers and whiners, complaining critics buzzing with their latest accusations and opinions. The world is changed by people who have been transformed by Christ, not small-minded critics. Be an encourager instead.

HANDLING A TOXIC RELATIONSHIP

To deal with toxic people effectively, you need an approach that enables you, across the board, to control what you can and eliminate what you can't.

"I can do all things through Christ who strengthens me" (**PHILIPPIANS 4:13**).

1. Set limits and boundaries (especially with complainers).

"You have set a boundary that they may not pass over, That they may not return to cover the earth" (**PSALM 104:9**).

"When I fixed My limit for it, And set bars and doors; When I said, 'This far you may come, but no farther, And here your proud waves must stop!'" (**JOB 38:10-11**).

Complainers and negative people are bad news because they wallow in their problems and fail to focus on solutions. They want people to join their pity party so that they can feel better about themselves. People often feel pressure to listen to complainers because they don't want to be seen as callous or rude, but there's a fine line between lending a sympathetic ear and getting sucked into their negative emotional spiral.

A great way to set limits is to ask complainers how they intend to fix the problem. They will either quiet down or redirect the conversation in a productive direction.

2. Don't die in the fight.

"Finally, my brethren, be strong in the Lord and in the power of His might. Put on the whole armor of God, that you may be able to stand against the wiles of the devil" (**EPHESIANS 6:10-11**).

Live to fight for your life another day, especially when your foe is a toxic individual. In conflict, unchecked emotion can make you dig your heels in and fight the kind of battle that can leave you severely damaged. When you read and respond to your emotions, you're able to choose your battles wisely and only stand your ground when the time is right.

3. Rise above (conflicts, violence, troubles, quarrels, hardship, etc.).

"Set your mind on things above, not on things on the earth" (**COLOSSIANS 3:2**).

"He delivers me from my enemies. You also lift me up above those who rise against me; You have delivered me from the violent man" (**PSALM 18:48**).

Toxic people drive you crazy because their behaviour is so irrational. Make no mistake about it—their behaviour truly goes against reason. So, why do you allow yourself to respond to them emotionally and get sucked into the mix and irrational attitude?

Distance yourself from them emotionally. You don't need to respond to the emotional chaos—only the facts.

4. Be aware of their emotions.

"Do not be deceived: 'Evil company corrupts good habits'" (**1 CORINTHIANS 15:33**).

Maintaining an emotional distance requires awareness. You can't stop someone from pushing your buttons if you don't recognise when it's happening. Sometimes, you'll find yourself in situations where you'll need to regroup and choose the best way forward.

5. Don't let anyone limit your joy.

"For we dare not class ourselves or compare ourselves with those who commend themselves. But they, measuring themselves by themselves, and comparing themselves among themselves, are not wise" (**2 CORINTHIANS 10:12**).

When your sense of pleasure and satisfaction are derived from the opinions of other people, you are no longer in command emotionally. Affirm yourself; you don't need anybody to affirm, reform, or confirm you.

I'm fearfully and wonderfully made (**PSALM 139:14**).

Eye has not seen, ear has not heard, neither has it entered the heart of man what God promised us (**1 CORINTHIANS 2:9**).

While it's impossible to turn off your reactions to what others think of you, you don't have to compare yourself to others, and you can always take people's opinions with a grain of salt. That way, no matter what toxic people are thinking or doing, your worth comes from within YOU.

6. Focus on solutions, not problems.

"While we do not look at the things which are seen, but at the things which are not seen. For the things which are seen are temporary, but the things which are not seen are eternal" (**2 CORINTHIANS 4:18**).

Where you focus your attention determines your emotional state.

When it comes to toxic people, gazing at how crazy and difficult they are gives them power over you. No matter how troubling a difficult person is, focus on how you're going to go about handling them. This makes you more effective, putting you in control, and reduces stress when interacting with them.

7. Remember not.

"'Do not remember the former things, Nor consider the things of old'" (**ISAIAH 43:18**).

Be quick to forgive. Forgiveness requires letting go of what's happened so that you can move on. Don't be bogged down unnecessarily by the mistakes of others; let them go quickly and be assertive in protecting yourself from future harm.

8. Avoid negative self-talk.

"There we saw the giants (the descendants of Anak came from the giants); and we were like grasshoppers in our own sight, and so we were in their sight" (**NUMBERS 13:33**).

When we absorb the negativity of other people, we self-talk (the thoughts we have about our own feelings). Negative self-talk is unrealistic, unnecessary, and self-defeating. It sends you into a downward emotional spiral that is difficult to pull out of. You should avoid negative self-talk at all costs.

9. Have a good sleep.

"It is vain for you to rise up early, To sit up late, To eat the bread of sorrows; For so He gives His beloved sleep" (**PSALM 127:2**).

A good night's sleep makes you more positive, creative, and proactive in your approach to toxic people. It gives you the perspective you need to deal effectively with them.

10. Use your support system.

"Two are better than one, Because they have a good reward for their labor" (**ECCLESIASTES 4.9**).

To deal with toxic people, you need to recognise the strength of a good team around you. This means tapping into your support system to gain perspective on a challenging person. Everyone has someone at work or outside of work who is on their team, rooting for them and ready to help them get the best from a difficult situation. Identify these individuals in your life and make an effort to seek their insight and assistance when you need it.

Maybe you were molested and abused.

Maybe you've been through a painful divorce, separation, or child custody battle.

Maybe you were wounded by the decision of your organization.

Maybe negative words were spoken against you by your teacher, lecturer, or parents.

God wants to heal and deliver you today—right now.

Lift your hands to heaven.

The Father wants to put you back together again—better, stronger, wiser, and greater.

Chapter Nine

FIXING A TOXIC RELATIONSHIP

TOXIC RELATIONSHIP SIGNS AND THE FIX

Do you find yourself in a toxic relationship and think that you might be the cause?

Toxic relationships are unhealthy relationships that cause ongoing emotional pain for those involved.

In order for you to know if you're the problem in your relationship or if there's something else going on, follow these 25 signs that may point to you being the issue:

1. YOU'RE ALWAYS THREATENING TO BREAK UP

If you're wondering whether you're the problem in your toxic relationship, then ask yourself this:

Are you constantly threatening to leave?

If the answer is "yes", then my answer is "yes" too. You are the problem in your toxic relationship.

How do you expect to have a stable relationship when there is a constant possibility that you'll bolt as soon as things get a little bit difficult or you don't get what you want?

The Fix

Be considerate with your words. Show kindness and consideration.

2. YOU ALWAYS FIND THINGS TO CRITICISE YOUR PARTNER ABOUT

If you feel like you're the problem in your toxic relationship, try this little exercise.

Write down all the things you said about your partner that you later regretted.

Be honest with yourself.

If you don't have any regrets, then you're probably not the problem.

If you have regrets or are overly and unjustly critical of your partner, you may be contributing to the toxicity in your relationship.

But what if you could change into someone less toxic?

The truth is, most of us never realise how much power and potential lies within us.

We become bogged down by continuous conditioning from society, the media, our education system, and more.

The reality we create becomes detached from the reality that lives within our consciousness.

In fact, many of us are self-sabotaging our love lives without realising it!

And one of the ways you're sacrificing your love is by finding things to criticise your partner about.

Far too often, we fall into codependent roles of saviour and victim to try to "fix" our partner, only to end up in a miserable, bitter routine.

The Fix

- You can't fix everyone.
- Speak kind words and show appreciation.
- Compliment and brag about your spouse.

3. YOU ASSUME THE WORST ABOUT YOUR PARTNER

Do you always assume the worst of your partner?

Do you have a hard time giving them the benefit of the doubt?

If you have answered "yes" to both questions, then you might be the cause of your toxic relationship.

You see, if there's no trust or faith between a couple, it's inevitable that conflicts and fights will arise due to misinterpretation and misunderstanding.

The Fix

A healthy relationship is based on trust and faith. No one can give that to you; it has to come from within.

4. YOU KEEP SCORES OF MISTAKES AND GRIEVANCES

Are you always able to recall past mistakes and grievances?

If you're unable to let the past go and you're unable to forgive your partner, then it's going to be very difficult to move forward with your relationship and your life.

There's only so much a person can take before walking away from a toxic relationship.

The Fix

Unless you learn to focus on the present and the future and let bygones be bygones, you risk losing your partner.

5. YOU NEVER SEEK COUNSELLING OR SPEAK TO A RELATIONSHIP PASTOR ABOUT YOUR SITUATION

Always love to keep things to yourself, probably because of arrogance or low self-esteem. Too proud to ask for help.

The Fix

- No person is an island.
- Ask, seek, and knock for help.
- Ask and receive. Seek and find. Knock and the door will open.

6. YOU BLAME YOUR PARTNER FOR EVERYTHING

Are you unable to admit when you're wrong?

If you always find fault with your partner, then chances are that you are the one causing tension and frustration in your relationship.

Finding faults is a way of trying to control the outcome or get revenge for something that went wrong in the relationship.

If this happens often enough, it can lead to an unhealthy pattern where one person constantly finds fault with their partner without actually offering any solutions on how they could improve things.

Everyone makes mistakes, but if you think that your partner is the only one who makes mistakes in your relationship, you're the problem.

The Fix

- Ditch the blame game.
- It's important not only for individuals but also for couples to be able to set aside those feelings and focus on what truly matters. Spend time and enjoy life together.

7. YOU'RE A GREAT MANIPULATOR

An obvious sign of a toxic person is that they are a great manipulator.

Manipulation is a toxic behaviour because it's wrong to use others for your own means.

So, ask yourself, are you constantly manipulating your partner to get what you want?

If you answered "yes" to this question, chances are that you're turning your partner into an object instead of a person.

The Fix

- Be a team player and builder.
- See the gifts and skills in your spouse.
- See the good in other people.

8. YOU'RE ADDICTED TO DRAMA

If you often find yourself in a fight and if your relationship is always on the verge of breaking up, then it might be time to recognise that drama has become an unhealthy part of your life.

If you're addicted to drama, it's inevitable that your relationship will become toxic and destructive.

The Fix

In order to have a healthy relationship with someone else, you must be able to communicate without fighting constantly or being jealous of each other all the time.

Drama has no place in a happy relationship.

9. YOU HAVE A MAJOR SUPERIORITY COMPLEX

Do you think you're better than everyone?

Do you think you're better than your partner?

Well then, I have news for you. You might be the reason for your toxic relationship.

Turns out that toxic people have superiority complexes that can include verbal put-downs, controlling behaviours, negative body language, and aggressive actions.

People with these types of personality traits like to dominate others.

They may create an illusion of power by fostering chaos, or they may be intensely jealous of those who command respect from others in order to feel validated.

A toxic person is always very condescending and often finds that they're in the right at all times.

The Fix

- In honour of preferring one another.
- Celebrate one another.
- Correct in love
- Speak the truth in love.

10. YOU OVERANALYSE EVERYTHING

If you're constantly worried that something will go wrong and are overanalysing every situation, you could be the problem in your relationship.

When you're in a relationship with someone, it's normal to worry about the future. There will always be uncertainties and unknowns that can cause concern.

But if you find yourself constantly worrying and stressing over everything, it could be that you are the issue in your relationship.

The Fix

- Do not analyse every decision or event that happens or doesn't happen in the relationship. Instead, focus on the present moment and how your partner is feeling.

- If there are some things that need addressing, take care of them without focusing so much on what may happen next.

- This will help both of you have a better time in the present moment and leave room for more possibilities for the future.

11. YOU DON'T RESPECT YOUR PARTNER'S BOUNDARIES

There are certain boundaries that are necessary for a relationship to function, and most people are aware of what those boundaries are.

Does this sound new to you?

Do you find that you are constantly disrespecting your partner's boundaries?

This could be because you don't realise what your boundaries are.

The Fix

- Observe your behaviour.

- Talk to your partner about it.

- Ask them how they feel.

- Ask them to tell you when you cross the line.

- This is very important because failing to respect boundaries can lead to a toxic relationship.

12. YOU'RE SELF-ABSORBED

Self-absorbed individuals tend to take everything personally and think the world revolves around them.

Because of this, they often lack empathy and make decisions on a whim rather than taking the time to consider what is best for everyone.

If you find yourself constantly thinking about yourself and your problems, it could be that you are the issue in your relationship.

The Fix

- Focus on your partner and their feelings.
- If you learn to do this, it will benefit all your relationships in life, whether with family members, friends, or colleagues.
- Remember that you're not the only one with feelings.

13. YOU HAVE A TEMPER

If you are constantly lashing out at your partner and can't contain your anger, then you're the reason you're in a toxic relationship.

When people have a temper, it becomes difficult for them to contain their thoughts and feelings.

This also causes them to lash out at whoever is closest to them.

The Fix

- Learn how to let go of your anger.
- Calm down. Seek peace. Experience joy. Relax. Be sober, be vigilant.
- Live humbly.

14. YOU'RE LETTING YOUR PARTNER DO ALL THE WORK.

You never want to get your hands dirty, so you let your partner do all the work in the relationship.

Whether it's getting stuff around the house done, taking care of the kids, bringing home the bacon, or initiating things in the bedroom, you leave it all to your partner.

If you think your relationship has become toxic, you're right, and the reason is your behaviour.

The Fix

Begin by actively participating in your relationship. Take the initiative to do something. Show your spouse that you care! Be involved. Make a difference.

15. YOU STONEWALL YOUR PARTNER

Do you find yourself starting to shut down mid-argument? Do you suddenly stop communicating and retreat?

Refusing to communicate with another person can have hurtful and frustrating effects.

Shutting down during an argument is called "stonewalling" and is also known as "the silent treatment".

It's not only harmful to a relationship, but it's toxic.

If you find yourself doing this often, then your relationship is in trouble.

The Fix

- Instead of stonewalling your partner, open yourself up to communication.
- Listen to their side of the story and give yours.
- I know it can be difficult to manage all the emotions that arise during an argument, but if you want your relationship to move forward, you have to be able to communicate effectively.

16. YOU DON'T STAY ON TOPIC WHEN YOU ARGUE

Do you sometimes find that you're having a heated conversation about one thing, and suddenly, it goes rogue, and you bring up something that upset you years and years ago?

You can't expect to have a productive relationship with someone unwilling to stay on topic during an argument.

This is toxic behaviour because it encourages arguing and fighting.

You begin to see all arguments as battles, and the discussion quickly devolves into name-calling, insults, and general aggression.

The Fix

- There's no point in talking about what happened years ago when you're already fighting about something unrelated.

- It's not good for anyone, that's for sure! The past is a spent cheque.

17. YOU IGNORE PROBLEMS

Do you find it easier to ignore problems in your relationship than to deal with them?

If you ignore your partner's red flags, then it's not surprising that you may find yourself in toxic situations time and time again.

Ignoring problems can snowball into a major problem in your relationship.

The Fix

- If you want a healthy relationship, you should be making an effort to discuss problems with your partner instead of ignoring them.

- If you're willing to put forth an effort to discuss problems with your partner, then the chances of an argument arising or trust declining are reduced or removed.

18. YOU'RE ADDICTED TO SOCIAL MEDIA

The problem of the modern-day woman and man—social media!

Sometimes, we spend so much time scrolling through our news feeds and social media that we neglect our relationships at home.

This is not good, especially in long-term relationships.

The Fix

It's okay to engage in social media from time to time, as long as you make sure to spend quality time with your partner.

19. YOU'RE LOSING FRIENDS

Have you ever noticed that a lot of your friends seem to be disappearing?

They've stopped texting you and hanging out with you as much.

If this sounds familiar, then chances are you're toxic.

What does it mean for someone to be toxic? It means that their behaviour is so upsetting and unapproachable that people stop being around them due to these behaviours.

You might not see yourself as toxic, but if you are causing a lot of drama or have lost many friends over time, it could be possible that you're toxic.

The Fix

- Value people and friendship
- Be tolerant and honour friendship
- Honour and celebrate your spouse.

20. YOU ONLY THINK ABOUT YOURSELF

Do you often put yourself first? Are you always thinking about yourself?

Do you have time to think about your partner's needs versus your own needs when a disagreement arises?

Toxic people are more concerned with their needs and wants than they are with the needs and wants of other people.

Toxic people may have a good idea of what other people need, but they aren't focused on others—they're only focused on themselves.

The Fix

- Be considerate and selfless.

- Learn to sacrifice for your spouse.
- If only you can meet the needs of others, yours too will be met.

21. YOU'RE CONTROLLING

Do you feel like you have to be in control?

It can be hard to admit when you have been the toxic person in a relationship.

People always want to believe that they're not toxic, which is why it's so important to know the signs that you are toxic and take steps to change your behaviour if necessary.

Toxic people are also known for being manipulative and controlling.

They use guilt trips, intimidation tactics, and emotional blackmail to get what they want from others.

The Fix

- Maybe it's time to take a hard, long look at yourself.
- Bring out the best in your spouse.

22. YOU NEVER HOLD YOURSELF ACCOUNTABLE

Do you always blame your partner for anything that goes wrong?

Is nothing ever your fault?

Toxic people may not be aware that they are toxic. They might not even realise that they are doing anything wrong.

However, in a relationship, it can be hard to admit that you are toxic when every time there is a disagreement or conflict, you put the blame on the other person and try to manipulate them.

If this sounds like you, it may indicate that something is very wrong with how you view yourself and interact with others.

The Fix

Take responsibility for what is happening in your life and, by extension, with everyone around you.

23. YOU'RE BOSSY

You're bossy, and you have a tendency to order other people around.

Your partner is not happy with this behaviour because it puts them in the position of having to do what you say, no matter how unreasonable or unfair your requests are.

Bossy people often struggle in relationships. Bossy people are often unhappy and frequently end up in unhappy marriages.

The thing is, many of them don't even know it! They think they're just taking charge, but their actions are actually making their partner feel like less of an equal.

The Fix

- You need to be more considerate if you want your relationship to work out. Team spirit and efforts are required.
- You're not a lone ranger.
- You're built for community.

24. YOU'RE ALWAYS IN A BAD MOOD

Do you feel like nothing ever goes right?

Are you always in a bad mood?

Well then, it's no wonder your relationship is toxic!

Bad moods can be so destructive that they lead to resentment and distrust.

It's possible that you have been carrying around a lot of negativity, and your partner is picking up on it.

Negativity is infectious.

Sometimes, the more toxic we are, the harder it is for us to see when our behaviour has an impact on others in our lives.

The Fix

Start working on your view of the world.

Take some time to focus inward and figure out what's causing this negativity, so you can start working towards a change.

Be more positive.

Get excited and be joyful.

Laughter is good medicine as a broken spirit dries up the bone

Joy is contagious

Be of good cheer, Jesus overcame the world already

25. YOU SELF-SABOTAGE FOR NO REASON

If you have a tendency to self-sabotage, then it's no surprise that you have problems in your relationship. Self-sabotage leads to self-destruction.

The reason you self-sabotage is that you don't think you deserve to be happy.

You believe that you are not good enough or worthy of happiness.

You may also think that your life is too difficult for someone like you to be happy.

The Fix

Your belief system must change as it becomes clear to you that there are many people in similar circumstances who have managed to find happiness despite how hard their lives were, so why can't you?

Chapter Ten

SOUL TIES

You have a spirit, soul, and body.

Soul ties are not merely about sexual relations, but all relational.

Inside the soul are your will, intellect, mind, and emotions.

Soul ties are places where we are connected to another person in the soul realm. It can create spiritual warfare and be a place where we cannot seem to obtain freedom. Breaking soul ties could be the missing element to your deliverance.

If you're still thinking of certain people you had a relationship with after you've left each other.

If you're still being haunted by what they said or did to you.

If you're struggling to move on and have a fresh start in life or in a relationship, and are unable to be emotionally free.

If you find it hard to stop checking the social media of those who left you.

If you're still stuck in the past and you avoid places where you'll meet people from your past.

These mean you're bound by an unhealthy soul tie.

One of the soul ties people often overlook is that of rejection, lust, and control. If you feel these things are out of character for you or anything in which you are currently struggling is not like you, discern a soul tie.

As the old adage goes, "We become who we hang around with." That's true in both the natural and spiritual. If you have never struggled with rejection and you notice an area of your life in which you are now feeling rejected, evaluate the relationships in your life and see if someone has a spirit of rejection. Relationships with people are where a soul tie can manifest, either good or bad.

Generational lines are additionally a place where we can inherit a soul tie. It is not always about breaking the generational curse, but in close family relationships, we need to sever the soul tie. This does not mean ending a relationship with a family member but rather breaking any unhealthy soul ties, such as anger or irritability. If you are having a difficult time being set free from your mother's control, then try severing a soul tie of control. It is a generational curse if you inherited it and are manifesting it, but it is a soul tie if your mother is still controlling you and you can't break free.

Soul ties can afflict us as we covet a person, idolise them, or begin to have lustful feelings toward them. They can enter through trauma, a controlling, emotionally abusive relationship or a ministry relationship in which you were close but then fell into being controlled and victimised.

We can't merely speak out, "All soul ties be gone in Jesus' name." We must do our part to break the agreement and renounce any known or unknown activity we have in our lives. Praying audibly to cancel the presence in the spiritual realm is an effective way to do so.

FREEDOM FROM SOUL TIES

1. Recognise what it is.

Ask the Holy Spirit for discernment on the root and core issue of your problem. The spirit of man is the candlelight of the almighty, searching all onwards.
JOB 20:27

2. Responsibility.

Take responsibility for what you recognise, what has been exposed, or what the Holy Spirit has convicted you of regarding this situation. Lest satan take advantage of us for we are not ignorant of his devices **2 CORINTHIANS 2:11**. Everyone shall bear his own burden Galatians 6:5

3. Repent for what you recognise.

Repent for the responsibility, repent for idolising, repent for being in a victimised relationship, repent for premarital sex, or repent for idolising a leader. Blood of Jesus cleanses from all unrighteousness. 1 John 1:7-9

4. Remove.

Remove objects from your life in correlation to this relationship. Remove pictures, gifts, jewellery, clothes. Ask the Holy Spirit to reveal them to you. Do a spiritual housecleaning. Destroy their power in the name of Jesus. **PHILIPPIANS 2:10-11**

5. Renounce.

Speak against and cancel the operation of the feelings or ties you see, such as idolisation, co-dependency, Jezebel, control, or manipulation. Erase all their activities and operations using the blood of Jesus. Colossians 2:14

6. Refuse.

Resist and refuse when it tries to come back. Cast down every imagination and high thing; cast down the thought (**2 CORINTHIANS 10:3-5**).

7. Rejoice.

Praise God for your freedom. Be of Good cheer, Jesus has overcome (**JOHN 16:33**).

8. Release.

Extend the ministry of deliverance and find another captive to set free. Release forgiveness to the people who hurt you. In the name of Jesus, we cast out devils (**MARK 16:17**).

9. Receive.

Receive the forgiveness and restoration Jesus wants to give you. Bless the Lord oh my soul who forgave all our sins (**PSALM 103:3**).

10. Respect.

Respect others and set healthy boundaries (**EPHESIANS 4:32**).

PRAYER

We must break every agreement with every soul tie, including those from generational bloodline.

Break, sever, and render inactive all curses and soul ties active in the spiritual and natural. In the name of Jesus.

Bind, rebuke and cancel all curses on your health, emotions and bloodline.

Speak and decree redemption from the curse, and that no weapon formed against you, etc {add to list} shall prosper.

Take authority over every soul tied in the spiritual realm; declare them null and void.

Cancel every effect of the soul ties by the blood of the Lamb.

Decree that all known and unknown soul ties, curses and demons are evicted, and any associated demonic spirits are cast out and evicted now, in Jesus' name!

ROOT SOURCES FOR DERAILED SEXUAL DEVELOPMENT

Many today find themselves infested with strongholds of sexual bondage and wonder how it could have happened. They've tried every way they know to get free, but nothing has worked. That may be because they haven't properly identified the roots and seriously engaged the Almighty God to lead them from deliverance to freedom.

Let's look at MAJOR INFLUENCES that lead to sexual bondage and brokenness.

1. Improper Role Modelling by Authority Figures

We were designed to take on the attributes of those in authority over us—absorbing their values, behaviours, and customs. It is built into our nature.

Those who grow up with dysfunctional parents or who live in other harmful environments will eventually grow to resent their lot in life and will often blame God for causing them to be born into such a situation. They will see God as unfair and uncaring, and may nurse a stronghold of anger that they draw upon to justify sinful lifestyles.

2. Inherited Generational Sins

The Bible is very clear that the sins of the fathers are passed down to the third and fourth generations of those who hate God. Very negative pattern. This is a strange concept because it seems to unfairly penalise children for sins committed by their parents or grandparents. It is a picture of how iniquity works in "covenantal" relationships.

God has made a way of escape; however, for that child who decides they are no longer going to follow in such sinful ways and who turns to the Lord to be set free. The Bible says that God will break the curse of the fathers from that generation and it will be destroyed.

In ministering to them, we must challenge such persons to:

- renounce the sinful line of their parents;
- declare that they are no longer going to participate in such works of iniquity;
- ask God to break and destroy the curse that is over them and set them free from the resultant bondage and brokenness.

3. The Influence of Teachers

A third major influence on improper sexual development in a growing child can be his or her teachers. If they fill their minds with lies, they will believe them. If they teach them that the Word of God is wrong, they will accept it, even against the witness of their conscience.

Some teachers affirm the wrong things, such as sexual promiscuity, trans or homosexual tendencies, rebellion against parents or unbelief. Worse still, a teacher who sexually molests a student causes great damage. It is the comparison and contrast of such factors with authority that makes the deception so destructive.

4. The Influence of Friends

If our friends exert a godly influence on us, we will tend to conform to their thinking and behaviour. Similarly, if they fill our minds with sinful knowledge and entice us with things that feed our fleshly nature, we will tend to mimic that influence in order to become accepted by them.

Friends can also cause us to form negative self-perceptions. They are often highly competitive and wield power through criticisms, intimidation, comparisons, gossip, etc. The more we look up to and admire our accusers, the more power their words have over us to create negative self-perceptions and behaviours.

5. The Influence of Heroes

Face it — our early years are spent identifying with and trying to become like our heroes. Because our culture is steeped in idolatry, sports figures, rock stars, media stars, and admired friends have an enormous power to sway our self-perceptions.

The "fall" of a hero provides the ammunition we need to justify our own fall. We say to ourselves, "If my hero turns to substance abuse or immorality in times of pain or sadness, then who am I to resist those same temptations?" In fact, "If the one who has embodied everything I have ever dreamed of being finds comfort and justification in sinful behaviour, then it must be okay!"

6. The Influence of Outsiders

Many kids have the unfortunate experience of meeting outsiders who do great damage to their sense of identity. A man who rapes a boy can be the cause of later sexual identity confusion or paedophilia in that boy. The one who shares pornography with a child can be the catalyst for a host of sexual obsessions, depending on variables like:

- age of exposure
- kind of pornography

- individual reaction in the soul and spirit of that child
- spiritual and emotional health of the child

Abuse by outsiders can be especially traumatising to those with a sensitive nature. They are plunged into a dark and secret world of fear where their sense of well-being and moral equilibrium are harshly compromised, and without apparent remedy.

7. The Influence of the Media

The greatest negative influence in our culture today is the media. In the secrecy of his bedroom, any five-year-old can view the most perverted pornography ever envisioned by the mind of man. Child and other hardcore pornography can be accessed on gigantic platforms like Facebook and X (formerly Twitter). Yet, no one seems to care!

Even cartoons by Disney, action movies by Marvel, TV programmes by Nickelodeon, and other sellers and promoters of children's media now feature positive depictions of heroes who live immoral lives.

All of this wreaks horrible damage to a child's mind, heart, and moral development.

8. The Influence of Self-Judgements

Self-judgements are natural byproducts of self-hatred forged in us by critical, legalistic authority figures. The result is that we become our own worst judges when facing failure. We condemn ourselves in expectation of the condemnation (real or imagined) that we believe will come our way.

Eventually, we reach such an emotionally damaged state that we purposely sin out of anger at being so sparsely affirmed and so harshly judged. Feeling justified, we throw temper tantrums over being given the impossible task of living a righteous life in our own strength.

The core sin is often twofold: failing to honour our parents because of their failings and refusing to believe in God's goodness. We presume that our judgement of the case is more valid than God's (**JOB 38:4**), and we believe that we are wiser than God (**1 CORINTHIANS. 1:20**), which is the cardinal sin of pride (**PROVERBS. 16:18**).

The fundamental error is that we choose to believe what our experiences say about God and our value in His eyes rather than what God actually says, thinks and feels.

9. The Influence of Childhood Vows

When we are hurt, we react from an immature sense of justice. We desire justice but know nothing of grace. And so, we condemn, hold grudges, pass sentences, dishonour, and make vows against those who have caused our pain—vows that remain hidden in our subconscious for decades before emerging under the convicting work of the Holy Spirit.

10. The Influence of the Sinful Heart of Man

A major source of improper sexual development is the evil heart of man (**MARK 7:20-23**). We are born with it, which is why we must be born again in order to enter the kingdom of God (**JOHN 3:3**). Parents, teachers, friends, heroes and strangers may be major contributors to our sexual sin issues, but they build on a foundation that we alone are accountable for—a human heart that is complicit with sin.

Being born again by receiving Jesus Christ as Lord and Saviour is the start of fixing the problem. When we give our hearts and lives to Him, a supernatural change takes place within us. We become born from above and receive a new heart!

11. The Influence of the Demonic Realm

Satan and his demons are a poisonous force for abnormal childhood development. Their influence is derivative, opportunistic, and fuelled by lies. They use the ground that we (or those who have covenantal influence over us) give them to worsen the damage caused by sinful choices.

Being demonised is not so much a matter of territorial occupation as it is about the degree of influence. A demonised person can come to Christ and receive deliverance, but they can also surrender ground to the demonic realm through sinful acts.

Demonising spirits gain influence over us according to the degree and length of participation in a sin. This is particularly true of knowing, wilful, and defiant sins. This makes the likelihood of a demonic outcome increase significantly.

It is common for a victim of abuse to make bitter judgements and vows or to pass condemning sentences against God and others. Although such reactions may be understandable, they remain sinful and allow demons to gain influence. Repentance and forgiveness are crucial.

Demons may gain ground if a child's legal head "uncovers" him or her. If the father or mother abuses the child, for example, his or her spiritual covering is compromised, enabling demonic powers to become involved. Believing children have recourse to God for His covering, but they often refuse to go there out of anger at Him for having allowed the abuse to happen.

We may attract demonic powers by viewing sin, however innocently. Many sex addicts tell of how their first exposure to pornography, though completely innocent, created a bondage to such images. Many will tell similar stories of innocently glancing into a window and seeing someone undressed and becoming obsessed with viewing others in the same secretive way.

We may also attract demonic powers by toying with the tools of the demonic realm, however innocently, such as hypnotism, Ouija boards, Eastern meditation, or astrology. In any healing or transformation process, it is essential to examine the person's beliefs and actions to determine if any ground has been ceded to the enemy. If so, we should ask the person to "renounce Satan and all of his works" before praying for deliverance.

The process of getting freed from sexual sin and bondage is a matter of uncovering (with God's help) the ground Satan has gained and removing that ground with the tools God has given us (Luke 10:19).

FINDING FREEDOM FROM DEMONIC OPPRESSION

Freedom often comes in multiple stages, especially for those who have suffered serious, multi-tiered, long-term demonisation.

1. Identify the powers & cast them out!

When saved from a life of immorality, one of the first areas that God addressed was demonic strongholds. Name the demons according to the sin they were tempting someone to commit, and cast them out in Jesus' name.

Many need seasoned believers to pray for them through such deliverance; however, it is important to listen carefully to the Holy Spirit for exactly what He wants you to do.

2. Enter into a lifestyle of worship.

At the Lord's direction, fill the air with love songs whose words were directed to Him. Demons cannot stand the worship of God, so if you marinate your life with intimate worship, these levels of demonic powers will leave on their own.

3. Seek help from mature believers who know how to minister from the leading and power of the Holy Spirit.

Attend deliverance and inner healing classes, conferences, and home fellowship groups where hands are laid while praying against hidden strongholds.

FINDING FREEDOM FROM A BROKEN IDENTITY

As you pursue an intimate relationship with Him, God will reveal your true identity through His Word, the encouragement of believers, and direct revelation to your soul.

Although the perception of one's identity is initially shaped through life's experiences and the opinions of others, we must choose whose opinion we're going to believe—man's or God's. If we accept God, He will engrave it in our hearts, and we'll be transformed into His image.

When we receive new hearts, God doesn't take away free will. The desires and temptations of the old nature remain an option, and we must make daily choices as to which heart we want to live from. We can pursue transformation into a more complete image of God (**1 PETER. 2:4-5**), life changing, or we can return to the ways of the old man which are destructive.

Right choices are a function of our love for God (**1 JOHN 4:19**). The degree of our love for God will be based on how diligently we pursue Him and are thereby exposed to His transforming glory and grace (**2 CORINTHIANS. 3:18**).

The development of bondage and brokenness has nothing to do with sex on its own. It is only the symptom of these deeper issues. If you have seen yourself in any of these root sources for improper sexual development, pursue an intimate relationship with God. Let Him be your healer, your righteousness, and your power source over sin.

Chapter Eleven

MARRIAGE AND ANGER MANAGEMENT

Countless number of people have lost their marriages because of anger. Some have lost their children, jobs, and health—all because they let this ONE emotion get out of control and take over their entire lives. What they need is to be set free from the bondage of bitterness, unforgiveness, rivalry, rejection and resentment.

ANGER DEFINED

One thing is for certain about anger: it doesn't feel the same to everyone. In fact, its definition may change depending on whom you ask.

Anger is defined as a strong, intense feeling of displeasure, hostility, or indignation resulting from a real or imagined threat, insult, injustice, or frustration to you or others who are important to you.

There's a lot packed into that definition! Let's break it down and take a look at it phrase by phrase:

1. ANGER IS INTENSE

Countless numbers of things in life can cause you to feel upset or frustrated. If not checked and addressed promptly, feelings of anger can intensify and persist long after the initial moment.

2. ANGER IS A FEELING

God, who created every aspect of our being for our good, made us feel and express emotions. He created us with a capacity to feel love, joy, and peace. The Lord also allows us to experience frustration, hurt, hate, and fear. He gave us specific emotions to help us intuitively, instinctively, and immediately recognise danger, injustice, and evil intent.

3. ANGER ENCOMPASSES OTHER FEELINGS

Emotions associated with anger are usually ones of displeasure, hostility, or indignation. All these are negative feelings, though that doesn't necessarily mean they're wrong. They're legitimate emotions, but they don't need to be expressed in negative behaviours.

4. ANGER COMES IN RESPONSE TO A THREAT—REAL OR IMAGINED

Each of us has a built-in fight-or-flight mechanism gifted to us by God for our human survival. And when we feel wronged or hurt in some way, our instinctive response is most often one of anger.

5. ANGER CAN FOLLOW A THREAT OF LOSS

You can become angry over a threat aimed at you personally or at someone important to you.

Our emotions are never to rule over us. We're to be the masters of our responses and reactions.

He who is slow to anger is better than the mighty, And he who rules his spirit than he who takes a city (**PROVERBS 16:32; NKJV**).

The moment we feel the intense emotion of anger, the first thing we must ask ourselves is, How should I respond? Ideally, our emotions will be filtered through a will that's bent toward God's purposes and commandments. However, if the filter has been damaged or never been put in place, emotions will usually give rise to unchecked behaviour. Also, emotions not subjected to godly thinking tend to run haywire and cause great damage in the long run.

THREE CORE TRUTHS ABOUT ANGER

In addition to a solid definition, we need to understand three core truths about anger and how it's manifested in our world.

1. ANGER IS UNIVERSAL

Anger is a universal emotion. It affects every person, regardless of race, sex, nationality, or age, from a screaming toddler to an elderly person red in the face with rage. It affects the person who lives in the cold of the Arctic to the heat of the Sahara and the one from a war zone to a tropical paradise. Anger is an emotion known to all people. Regardless of how peaceful or passive a person might seem or desire to be, everyone gets angry at some point in life.

But the fact that everyone gets angry isn't a justification for it. The universality of anger isn't an excuse for getting angry, nor is it an excuse for failing to deal with it or failing to direct it toward godly goals.

2. ANGER IS PERSISTENT

Anger will not go away on its own. It doesn't die out. It must be rooted out. Dealing with anger—especially deep-seated anger—requires intentionality.

3. ANGER IS EPISODIC AND PERVASIVE

We're wise to differentiate between angry episodes and a pervasively angry nature.

Is there evidence that you're a chronically angry person? Are you angry about something nearly all the time, even if you wear a smile on your face and speak in a soft, calm voice?

There's a big difference between the person who feels anger as a response to a specific situation or circumstance and the one whose anger doesn't go away. If you're angry at the first step of a journey and are still angry a thousand miles later, you will likely live with pervasive anger.

The apostle Paul wrote to the Ephesians, *"Be angry, and yet do not sin"* (**EPHESIANS. 4:26**). He openly and directly admitted that anger exists, that it's part of everyone's emotional makeup—even the most mature and spiritually minded person—and that we all get angry from time to time.

If you build your identity on anything else, you'll struggle with insecurity your whole life. You can build your identity on your job, but you can lose your job. You can build your identity on how good-looking you are, but you may lose your good looks. You can build your identity on the person you married, but your spouse will eventually die. You can build your identity on being popular, but you're not always going to be popular.

If you build your identity on anything that can be taken away from you, you're going to be insecure, and insecurity is at the root of your anger. Until you start feeling secure about yourself, others will continue to push your buttons. When you know who you are and whose you are, people can't push your buttons. They can't get to you. Anger and insecurity go together. The more insecure you feel, the angrier you feel.

The Bible says in **PROVERBS 29:25 (MSG)**, *"The fear of human opinion disables; trusting in God protects you from that".*

When you get angry, your mouth just reveals what's inside your heart.

Take a good look and check this out:

- A harsh tongue reveals an angry heart.
- A negative tongue reveals a fearful heart.
- A boasting tongue reveals an insecure heart.
- An overactive tongue reveals an unsettled heart.
- A judgemental tongue reveals a guilty heart.
- A critical tongue reveals a bitter heart.
- A filthy tongue reveals an impure heart.
- An encouraging tongue reveals a happy heart.
- A gentle tongue reveals a loving heart, and
- A controlled tongue reveals a peaceful heart

ANGER'S LINK TO OTHER EMOTIONS & FACTORS

Anger has a way of linking itself to many other emotions—with the end result almost always negative.

Stick around and consider these combinations:

Anger + Hatred = Rage

Anger + Bitterness = Revenge

Anger + Worry = A Divided Mind

Anger + Confusion = Turmoil / Indecision

Anger + Insecurity = Manipulation / Control Tactics

Anger + Stress = Physical, Mental, or Emotional Breakdown / Burnout

Anger + Resentment = Retribution

Anger + Fear = Irrational Response

Anger + Sorrow = Disorientation / Inability to Function

Anger also tends to take on different forms depending on time, space, and situation.

Consider these combinations:

Anger + Urgency = Panic

Anger + Confinement = Explosive Behaviour

Anger + Constraint = Tantrum

Anger + Grief = Cloudy Thinking

Anger + Too Many Options = Poor Decision Making

ANGER ROOTS

The origin of anger exhibits fruits such as; Fury, rage, temper, annoyance, provocation, irritation, resentment, bitterness, and a show of strong emotions.

1. BLAME & SHAME

Who was the first person in the Bible to get angry?

When asked that question, most people reply, "Cain."

Without a doubt, he was a very angry man, but Cain wasn't the first person in the Bible who got angry.

Consider carefully what happened in the Garden of Eden. Adam found himself married to the most beautiful woman imaginable. His life was paradise. He had a close relationship with God, ruled over creation, and enjoyed constant renewal of life. Then one day, he took a bite of a forbidden fruit, and his entire world came crashing down. He was cast out of the garden and became destined to work by the sweat of his brow until the day he died.

Could it be possible that Adam was more than a little angry with the woman? Absolutely. How do we know that? Because he blamed Eve for what happened to them. When God confronted him in the garden, Adam responded,

"The woman whom You gave to be with me, she gave me from the tree, and I ate" (**GENESIS 3:12**).

The blame game finds its roots in anger. Ashamed and not wanting to take responsibility for what he'd done, Adam lashed out and placed the blame on Eve. And it's a pattern that continues to this day.

For Eve's part, she was also angry. When God confronted her about what she did, Eve played the blame game, too:

"The serpent deceived me, and I ate" (**GENESIS. 3:13**).

Blame is easy

...taking responsibility is hard.

Anger is easy

...self-control is hard.

Externally, we may become angry with others who tempt or entice us to do something morally wrong or against our better judgement. And we might become angry when someone lies, defrauds or preys on our vulnerability or weakness.

Internally, we may become angry with ourselves for being gullible, buying into a lie, or participating in a sinful act, even though we knew it was wrong. We blame ourselves and often feel shame—living disgraced, dishonoured, unworthy, or embarrassed in our own minds.

But God wants us to know there's a better way to react. When we're assured of our relationship with Him, we can take responsibility for our own actions and not fall into the "blame game" trap—whether blaming ourselves or others. And when we accept his forgiveness for our sins and extend that same forgiveness toward others, blame and shame have no power over us.

2. PRIDE

Most people are born with a desire to be number one. It's been part of our human nature since Adam and Eve rebelled against God in the Garden of Eden and introduced sin into the world.

Babies cry as a demand to be fed in their first hours of life. As they grow, they learn that crying and throwing tantrums "work"—it's a way to have their desires met. The sad truth is, some people are still throwing tantrums even when they're 20, 40, 60, or 80 years old. Why? Simply because they still want their own way. They want what they want when they want it, regardless of the needs or feelings of others. Pride is their driving force.

Whenever a person doesn't get what they deeply desire, anger is likely to arise. Whether it's jealousy, envy, greed, losing something closely tied to his identity, or being denied something he truly believes he needs, anger tends to be the result when things don't "go his way."

However, no one can have their way all the time and in every situation. Many people become angry when they don't have control over a desired situation or individual. And the anger of some can spin out of control when they realise they cannot and will not have control over God.

There are many examples of pride-related anger found throughout the Bible. Let's take a look at a few:

1 Cain and Abel

2. Herod and Hebrew infants

3. Herod and John the Baptist

4. Nabal and David

5. Jonah and Nineveh people

3. INSECURITY

(Feel you're not good enough & lack confidence)

The more insecure people are, the easier it is for them to feel anger. Why? Because insecurity is often related to feelings of low self-worth that come from:

- Rejection
- Fears (especially fear of loss)
- Disappointment
- Feelings of inadequacy

Not everyone who has these feelings becomes angry, but many people do. They blame themselves. They blame others. They feel shame. A deep-seated inner frustration develops, taking the form of anger. And, as stated previously, when the person begins to act out based on their emotions, the results are almost always negative.

Insecure people have difficulty establishing good, lasting relationships. They simply can't see how they could add value to anyone else's life. Also, lack of confidence can cause some people to withdraw from others, which can easily be mistaken for anger or an act of arrogance.

4. DREAMS DEFERRED OR DENIED

A brilliant person can be denied plans of greatness and become upset forever, with a heart full of bitterness and resentment.

The bitterness can spill over into every relationship developed, leaving feelings of rejection and isolation.

We must remember that when we hold on to our anger and bitterness, our entire lives will suffer from their poison.

5. LIES & COVER-UPS

Have you ever been angry when you discovered someone was talking negatively about you? Perhaps it was a rumour attacking your character or tarnishing your good name.

Anger based on rumours, partial truths, or full-blown lies can take you down a long, dark road of disappointment, frustration, and heartache. Confronting the truth may be painful, but always remember the alternative can be far worse.

6. BRAIN DYSFUNCTION

A root of anger that's more common than many people realise is brain dysfunction or mental illness.

Brain dysfunction may be the result of a degenerative disease or an accident. Or the brain may function improperly due to a chemical imbalance present from birth that may manifest itself as mental illness. It may even be self-inflicted through alcohol and drug use.

Dealing with anger as a result of brain dysfunction or mental illness is extremely difficult in marriage, friendship, and work relationships.

7. CHEMICAL ADDICTION

Even as we consider brain dysfunction, we're wise to recognise that certain chemicals are poison to the brain. Alcohol is one of them. A number of other drugs and medications are toxic to the brain when used in great quantity or over great lengths of time.

In a marital scenario, Abigail returned home to find Nabal hosting a lavish feast and appearing "very drunk" (1 SAMUEL 25:36).

We learn more about Abigail's wisdom when Scripture explains, "She did not tell him anything at all until the morning light" (1 SAMUEL 25:36). She waited until "the wine had gone out of Nabal" (1 SAMUEL 25:37), and then she told him what David had intended and what she'd done to avoid bloodshed.

If you or someone you love has a problem with drugs or alcohol, ask God to help you seek help and overcome it today.

CHARACTERISTICS OF ANGRY PEOPLE:

1. Tardiness

They tend to be tardy in an attempt to control a situation or draw attention to themselves in order to express anger.

2. Obstructive Behaviour in Groups

They fail to cooperate to the point that they are truly disagreeable. These individuals object to every idea, proposition, and solution suggested with an air of disdain.

3. Cynicism

They find fault in every person or situation.

4. Jabbing Jokes

They tell embarrassing stories with the intent of hurting the subject of the joke.

5. Disrupting Conversations

They feel a deep need to interject their opinion, even if it's off topic.

6. Sloppy Job Performance

They're often resentful to the point they no longer care about doing a good job. They're not motivated to give their best effort.

7. Loss of Enthusiasm

Deep down, they don't want to be happy. This very often translates into a down-in-the-mouth attitude. The angry person may withdraw from social settings or turn down invitations to public events. The angry person would rather brood than laugh.

8. Depression

What begins as a self-imposed lack of enthusiasm can end up as full-blown depression. Angry people often slide into periods of deep discouragement and despair, in part because they hate the fact that no one seems to take their anger as seriously as they do.

9. Procrastination

The angry person has little desire to start new things that require focus or creativity.

10. Eating Disorders

Angry people can overeat, undereat, or overexercise. They frequently find themselves facing obesity, anorexia, or bulimia.

11. Sexual Dysfunction

Many people have problems in their sexual lives because they're angry. When a person is angry and wants sex, what that person is doing is expressing anger to someone else through an act. Sex without love is just an act. Animals do that. It's damaging and can destroy a life and a marriage. That's how powerful and deceptive anger is. But when genuine, godly, intimate love is present, it's a whole different story.

ANGER COST

PROVERBS 15:18 (TEV): *"Hot tempers cause arguments, but patience brings peace."*

PROVERBS 29:22 (TEV): *"People with quick tempers cause a lot of quarreling and trouble."*

PROVERBS 14:17 (TEV): *"People with a hot temper do foolish things; wiser people remain calm."*

The Bible says, *"The fool who provokes his family to anger and resentment will finally have nothing worthwhile left. He shall be the servant of a wiser man"* (**PROVERBS 11:29 TLB**).

Whenever anyone loses their temper, they lose. You don't make it to the top if you're continually blowing your top.

The word "danger" is the word "anger" with the letter "d" in front. And anger is dangerous.

You could lose everything: your reputation, spouse, job, and health.

Medical research on the human heart has revealed that reducing hostility in your life can prolong your life.

Mom and Dad, listen, we may get a short-term payoff by motivating our kids through anger. They will comply out of fear, but in the long run, we'll lose because anger always alienates.

It turns people off rather than turning them on. And, instead of getting what you want, it causes people to become apathetic to your needs and angry at you.

MANAGING ANGER

One way to manage your anger is to come to grips with how much it is costing you.

He that is soon angry dealeth foolishly: And a man of wicked devices is hated (**Proverbs 14:17; KJV**).

A wrathful man stirreth up strife: But he that is slow to anger appeaseth strife (**PROVERBS 15:18; KJV**).

An angry man stirreth up strife, And a furious man aboundeth in transgression (**PROVERBS 29:22; KJV**).

He that troubleth his own house shall inherit the wind: And the fool shall be servant to the wise of heart (**PROVERBS 11:29; KJV**).

REFLECT BEFORE YOU RESPOND

When you're angry, don't respond impulsively. Delay is a great tool in controlling anger. I'm not saying delay indefinitely, or even beyond a day. The Bible says don't go to sleep when you're angry. I'm talking about delaying it for five minutes.

You need to reflect before you respond. When we get angry, we need to get in the habit of stepping back, waiting a few minutes, and then looking at the situation from God's point of view. Notice the Bible says a wise man lets his anger cool down (**PROVERBS 29:11**). So, "cool it" is a biblical term!

While you're cooling down, ask yourself three questions to help you understand why you are angry:

- Why am I angry?
- What do I really want?
- How can I get it?

Understanding the reason for your anger will give you greater patience and, perhaps, even the ability to overlook an offence (**PROVERBS 19:11**).

A fool uttereth all his mind: But a wise man keepeth it in till afterwards (**PROVERBS 29:11; KJV**).

The discretion of a man deferreth his anger; And it is his glory to pass over a transgression (**PROVERBS 19:11; KJV**).

Chapter Twelve

DEALING WITH ANGER

1. ADMIT YOUR ANGER TO GOD

It is true for many people that an angry response has become habitual. If this is the case for you, I recommend you talk to God. Tell Him, "Father, I confess that I don't know how to respond to emotional pain or rejection apart from anger. Show me a new way of handling life's difficult situations. Lead me to the right information and help me make the necessary changes. I trust You to help me break this habit of anger once and for all."

2. IDENTIFY THE SOURCE OF YOUR ANGER

Somebody once said, "I thought my husband was making me angry, but then I realised it wasn't really his actions that were triggering this emotion. It was a memory of my father's actions that had established a pattern of anger in my life." This is true for many people. Something their parents said in the distant past still rings as criticism in their ears. The "tape" goes round and round.

It's played and played again.

Such as,

You're worthless.

You were never wanted.

You'll never amount to anything.

You'll never have what you dream of having.

Your "recording" could be something your spouse said during an argument or what your teenager said before storming out of the house. The pain of these memories, coupled with a strong sense of rejection, can lead to inner turmoil that frequently manifests itself as anger.

Oftentimes, people will become angry about something that has nothing to do with you. However, they need to find someone to blame, so they transfer the blame to you. If this happens, you must address it quickly and properly.

Whether someone's anger is justified or unjustified, you can pray for that person to be healed emotionally and find peace. Ask God to help this individual let go of the anger and focus on positive things. Pray that God will move in the heart of the angry person to bring healing and joy. Finally, ask the Lord to bless and restore your relationship with that person.

3. GIVE UP YOUR RIGHTS TO ANGER

The way you address anger is a matter of your will. You can and must take authority over your emotions and choose to release the anger.

Don't try to justify your anger.

Don't make excuses for it.

Don't transfer it to or blame others.

Own up to your feelings through prayer: "God, help me to deal with this quickly and effectively. Don't let anger poison my soul."

"Anger is like spilling something on a clean white shirt. If you clean it quickly and properly, there's a good chance it won't become a lasting stain. But if you ignore it and wait too long to treat the stain, your garment will likely be ruined forever."

"But I have a right to be angry," a person might say. "If I don't speak up immediately, I'll lose my opportunity to let the other person know that I'm worthy of respect."

Or you may hear someone else explain, "I have a right to respond in a way that lets a person know I have a right to my own feelings and to express them in any way I want, including anger."

The truth is that you don't have any of these so-called rights. Completely surrendering your anger to God means you are giving up your "right" to get even with a person who wronged you or made you angry. You are saying, "I won't try to hurt you or seek payback." You are willing to forgive, no matter what the person did to you. And when you do surrender completely, you will find that God heals, blesses, and guides you in ways that are truly miraculous.

4. TAKE A TIME OUT

If someone or something makes you angry and you start seeing red, choose to visualise it in the shape of a stop sign. Imagine yourself at an intersection and come to a full, complete stop. Carefully consider all the directions your anger can go, then respond slowly and deliberately.

PSALM 103:8 says that God is *"slow to anger."*

JAMES 1:19 encourages everyone to be *"quick to hear, slow to speak and slow to anger."*

We must always remember that nearly every person has control over their thoughts, emotions, and responses at any given time. For the most part, we choose how we feel, what we think, and what we believe. When we find ourselves in situations that evoke anger, pausing to calm our emotions and seek the Lord is always the wisest course of action. As we pause to take a deep breath and bring our concerns before the Lord, He reveals the truth of our situation and, when asked in prayer, promises to show us the best way to respond, providing for us a way out in the best and godliest of ways.

As you move through life, encountering many people and situations that can evoke strong emotions, ensure that your response is always a godly one. Remember to rule your tongue. Don't speak too quickly, consider the cost, and take a much-needed time out when you need one.

5. GET TO THE ROOT OF THE PROBLEM

In many cases, a person's anger has nothing to do with what you have said or done. He's responding out of frustration, stress, insecurity, jealousy, fatigue, or something else that is entirely unrelated to his interaction with you. It is not uncommon for people to become angry when they allow themselves to get too hungry, lonely, or tired.

Listening to someone tell their story and allowing them to get to the root of the problem goes a long way to defusing anger. Sometimes, in recounting the offence, hurt, or rejection, a person is better able to see where their strong reaction and emotion have their roots. God uses others to help us "work our way" through any problem we have from the root to its solution, deepening our relationship with Him and others in the process.

6. VOICE YOUR ANGER TO THE ONE WHO CAN HELP YOU MOST

There is very little value in venting anger simply for the sake of doing so. Behavioural scientists have discovered that even after an individual screams into a pillow, most of the feelings of anger that have taken residence in that person remain. Expressing anger does not produce healing.

Take your anger to God. Get by yourself, on your knees, with your Bible open. Ask the Lord to show you why you're angry and what you can do to redirect your negative feelings into positive behaviour. He knows why you're angry. He knows your situation and circumstances. Trust Him to reveal the best way to identify, deal with, and let go of your anger.

As you read your Bible, focus on the words of Jesus in the four Gospels. Or turn to the book of Psalms for encouragement and peace. Practical, how-to advice is found in the book of Proverbs. And for guidance on victorious Christian living, open your Bible to any of Paul's writings, including Romans, Ephesians, and Philippians. As you take your concerns to the Lord and spend time with Him in prayer and study of His Word, you will find your anger dissipating as the Father heals your soul in "the light of His glory and grace."

7. REDIRECT YOUR ENERGY

Anger produces energy that can be redirected to countless good behaviours. Use your anger to do something useful and productive.

Wash and wax your car. If you're still angry after that, clean the interior.

Clean out a closet, the attic, the cupboards, or any other area of your home.

Weed your flower beds or till the soil in your vegetable garden. Don't have either? Plant one. It's amazing what planting something and watching it grow can do to calm you.

Go to the driving range and hit a large bucket of golf balls.

There's something therapeutic and beneficial about engaging in physical activity. It helps you blow off steam. And when you rechannel that negative energy in the right direction, it can prove to be profitable. Just think of all you can accomplish. So, get rid of it! Replace your anger with physical activity.

What about walking, running, swimming, hiking, or riding a bicycle? These activities are good for the body, but they do not require your complete attention.

What about doing a puzzle or reading a book? These are good for focusing the mind, but they are not activities that release pent-up physical energy. Choose an activity that engages both the mind and body in a healthful and productive way.

Intense anger has an element of confusion to it. In most cases, it is a free-floating emotion looking for a place to land. As a result, angry people often want to pound something with their fist or find an object to pick up and throw. Give your anger a positive focus. Expend that negative energy in a way that is productive...not destructive.

8. RESET YOUR PERSONAL, EMOTIONAL DIAL

The apostle Paul challenged the Ephesians to "put away" their anger (**EPHESIANS 4:31**). In the Greek, this phrase literally means to strip away or to lift up and toss away. In other words, the Bible commands that we remove anger completely from our hearts.

And if you are a believer, you have the power of the Holy Spirit within you to lay it down. All you need to say is, "God, I don't want this anger in my life, and I choose to lay it down by Your grace, love, and goodness."

Now, there are some other things you still need to address. That's not the end of the issue. But that's a major part of letting go of anger. You put it down. Get rid of it. Get rid of "bitterness and wrath and anger and clamor and slander … along with all malice" (**EPHESIANS 4:31**).

9. DETERMINE HOW YOU WILL RESPOND IN THE FUTURE

After any angry encounter, it's wise to decide how you will respond the next time you see that person. You may want to rehearse in your mind what you will say and how you will behave. Envision yourself in a similar situation or circumstance and ask yourself, 'What would I do differently?' How should I behave the next time something similar arises?

You might say, "But I don't know what kind of mood the other person will be in." His or her mood or behaviour doesn't matter. What matters is that you determine that you are going to greet that person with peace in your heart, a cheerful attitude, and a positive word. Do not let the mood or behaviour of other people dictate your responses to life. Choose how you will act.

Don't let another person affect the spring in your step or the twinkle in your eye.

Don't let anyone rob you of your smile.

Don't let someone else cause you to be discouraged or unhappy.

The more you mentally prepare yourself for the difficult experiences, the more peaceful you will be in times of anger or frustration (**PROVERBS 13:16**).

10. SET EMOTIONAL GOALS IN KEY RELATIONSHIPS

Relationships. We all have them. Some are great, some are strained, and some are just not working at all—no matter how hard we try. What do we do when dealing with the key relationships in our lives? A good place to start is discussing your relationships. You don't need to overanalyse them to the point of stifling normal, open communication and interaction. However, you should also refrain from discussing your feelings, hopes, dreams, and desires with those closest to you. And you certainly should spend some time learning about theirs. Find a happy balance.

Spend quality time alone with your spouse, each of your children, and your close friends. Point out positive aspects of the other person's character, attitude, and personality. Reflect on what your relationship has meant to you through the years. Talk about ways you can strengthen your marriage, your parent-child relationship, or your friendship. Express your desire to see your key relationships grow stronger.

Chapter Thirteen

MONEY (PROSPERITY) AND MARRIAGE

The love of money definitely is the root of all evil. Money problems are actually one of the causes of divorce. Many have health and no money. Some have money but no peace. Some have no money, no peace, no health. All kinds of issues in life. Eighty-five percent of married couples experience money stress regularly, with bills being the most common cause of concern.

There arc about four distinct money scripts, which can manifest in numerous thoughts that influence our behaviour such as:

MONEY AVOIDANCE:

- "I do not deserve money…
- Money corrupts people…
- It is hard to accept financial gifts from others…"

MONEY WORSHIP:

- "Things would get better if I had more money…
- You can never have enough money…
- Money is power…
- Money buys freedom…"

MONEY STATUS:

- "Money is what gives life meaning…
- Your self-worth equals your net worth…
- People are only as successful as the amount of money they earn…"

MONEY VIGILANCE:

- "You should not tell others how much money you have or make…
- It is wrong to ask others how much money they have or make…
- Money should be saved, not spent…"

Please answer all the following questions straight from the heart:

How did you grow up around money?

....

....

How did your parents or caregivers relate to money?

....

....

How does money make you feel?

....

....

Why do you buy the things you buy?

....

....

Over the course of your working life, where has your money gone?

....

....

If you had a magic wand, what would you change about your financial situation?

....

....

What do you believe about money?

....

....

SIGNS YOU NEED FINANCIAL BALANCE:

- You're having a hard time handling money on your own, whether it's putting together your own financial picture or recovering from financial stress.

- You have a hard time communicating with others about money.

- You're experiencing financial anxiety. This can manifest in various ways, potentially including avoiding bills or pretending to be blissfully ignorant of your financial situation.

- You self-sabotage when trying to take steps toward correcting bad behaviours because you don't believe you deserve financial stability or because you feel uncomfortable with having money.

UNDERSTANDING MONEY IN A HOSTILE FINANCIAL WORLD

1. PUT GOD FIRST IN YOUR FINANCES

Honor the Lord with your possessions, And with the firstfruits of all your increase; So your barns will be filled with plenty, And your vats will overflow with new wine (**PROVERBS 3:9-10; NKJV**).

The thought of giving up money can be very frightening if someone has not been delivered from or experienced freedom from financial difficulty and hardship. The thought of asking if the concept of tithing really makes sense? How could God expect one to live off only 90% of their income, especially if barely making ends meet?

Many are fearful that they would be unable to make ends meet if they commit to God. However, the reality is that they can't afford not to.

"Bring all the tithes into the storehouse, That there may be food in My house, And try Me now in this, says the Lord of hosts, If I will not open for you the windows of heaven and pour out for you such blessing that there will not be room enough to receive it" (**MALACHI 3:10**).

Trusting God with your finances requires a faithful commitment to God. It means even when your change is "strange", you will still commit to what God has already instructed you to do.

As soon as you decide to tithe and really trust God, there may be distractions that get you off track. This is just a test! Stay true to your commitment, and you will see God's blessings in your marital life and destiny. Your marriage will be full of unexpected provisions and breakthroughs.

2. PLAN FOR YOUR FINANCIAL FUTURE

How is your financial future?

Proverbs 21:5: God tells us the plans of the diligent will lead to profit, however, those who are hasty or fail to plan will certainly lead to poverty.

To experience financial healing, you must have a financial plan. This way, attacks of unexpected expenses, unemployment, natural disasters, illnesses, and other adverse financial events will not cause your financial house to be shaken.

THE POWER OF WRITING

It is essential to write your financial goals on paper. Please understand that there is something powerful about putting your thoughts on paper.

As you write out your plans and goals, God blesses you so much more! Habakkuk 2:2 instructs us to write the vision and make it plain so that he may run who reads it.

DECLARE AND DECREE

Wake up each morning, declaring that your financial goals will come to pass. Post your financial goals somewhere you can view them throughout the day. Whether you post them on your refrigerator or dressing mirror, allow your goals to serve as a constant reminder of where you are going. Seeing these visually can also encourage you when deciding whether to purchase a pair of shoes, tickets to your favourite sports game, or your morning coffee latte. Understand how making these small sacrifices may ensure your children's education is funded, reduce your financial burdens, or allow you the ability to live a financially healing lifestyle.

3. LET YOUR BUDGET INSPIRE YOU

You hear it every time and everywhere: spend within your budgets, but what does that really mean? Many people spend aimlessly without preparing a budget, and as a result, they usually fall short in their financial goals.

Budget

A budget is simply a list of expected income and expenses for a period of time. A budget should be prepared at the beginning of the month or periodically, with the understanding that it is a flexible and moving document. You should budget for all expected expenses. A budget serves as a roadmap to help reach financial goals.

LUKE 14:28-30 encourages budgeting:

For which of you, intending to build a tower, does not sit down first and count the cost, whether he has enough to finish it— lest, after he has laid the foundation, and is not able to finish, all who see it begin to mock him, saying, 'This man began to build and was not able to finish'?

Envision what your future budget will be. This gives you a clear vision to determine where you're headed, inspiration to keep pressing, knowing victory is assured, and a constant reminder that small sacrifices will provide big rewards in the future. Consider placing your inspiration budget somewhere you can see it every day.

More importantly, if you want to achieve victory over your financial life, consider taking steps toward living within your budget and creating an inspirational budget. You will see God do a great thing in your life.

4. BE PREPARED FOR WHAT TOMORROW BRINGS

Situations can arise that may put us in a fix and create financial uncertainties in life. The Bible admonishes us to plan. It refers to **PROVERBS 21:5:** *The plans of the diligent lead surely to plenty, But those of everyone who is hasty, surely to poverty.*

This also applies to all areas of our lives; hence, no matter what, commit to preparing yourself financially for the unexpected.

JAMES 1:5 tells us that we can ask God for wisdom, and He will generously provide it to us. This requires us to be good stewards of our finances and set aside a portion that comes into our possession.

On the first day of the week let each one of you lay something aside, storing up as he may prosper, that there be no collections when I come (**1 CORINTHIANS 16:2**).

Be prepared

MATTHEW 25:6-10 warns us about the consequences of being unprepared for the unexpected. We witnessed ten women who set out on the journey, but only half were able to conquer it. An unexpected expense shouldn't hinder our financial fulfilment.

We have to be prepared for whatever tomorrow brings.

5. YOU CAN BE THE LENDER AND NOT A BORROWER

Many times, we believe in God for certain areas of our lives but fail to believe in God for the possibility of being debt-free. Renew your mind to believe that you can live debt-free.

By divine inspiration, meditate on **PROVERBS 3:5-6:**

Trust in the Lord with all your heart, And lean not on your own understanding; In all your ways acknowledge Him, And He shall direct your paths.

Get creative

Create expected additional streams of income and be committed to reducing debt. Stay on course with a debt-free plan. This served as a reminder to help stay on course, and when tempted to purchase a "want," be reminded that in a few months going forward, you would have a zero-debt balance. Now, it is possible to be totally debt-free!

6. INVEST YOUR MONEY

"Then another came, saying, 'Master, here is your mina, which I have kept put away in a handkerchief. For I feared you, because you are an austere man. You collect what you did not deposit, and reap what you did not sow.' And he said to him, 'Out of your own mouth I will judge you, you wicked servant. You knew that I was an austere man, collecting what I did not deposit and reaping what I did not sow (LUKE 19:20-22).

The nobleman leaves money to each of his ten servants upon his departure. He instructs each of them to invest the money until he returns. Upon his return, he calls each of the ten servants to determine how much money each has gained by investment.

Be faithful

Just as in this passage, God requires us to be good stewards over all that He has placed in our care. It is our responsibility to ensure our gifts, talents, and, more importantly, our money grow. If we are not growing our resources, we are not exercising good stewardship over what God has given us.

Understanding whether to invest is a matter of aligning your financial goals with your time frame.

7. LET YOUR FINANCES BE DECENT AND IN ORDER

The true way to conquer finances is to first get a grip on them (1 CORINTHIANS 14:40).

This reminds us that everything we do must be done not only decently but in order.

We too must organise. Each month, we are bombarded with bills in our inbox, on our smartphone, or in our mail. And of course, without a sound system in place, we can easily be overwhelmed. If your bills have gotten the best of you and are stressing life out of your marriage, here are a few steps to help manage your monthly bills.

Having a system for your bills is key. A great idea is to pay your bills according to your pay schedule. For example, if you are paid on the 1st and 15th, you may want to pay your bills on the same dates.

For each financial document that comes into your possession, create a place for it. This may require setting up file folders for tax expenses, bank statements, insurance, monthly bills, and other financial documents that you may encounter. This way, if you need a document, these items can be easily accessible to help you in your financial journey.

8. BE FAITHFUL OVER A LITTLE

Throughout life, God will bless you with an infinite number of resources. You will be blessed with only so much money, time, assets, and talents. With each blessing God has given you, He expects you to be a good steward of what He has blessed you with.

Faithfulness Always Creates Fruitfulness

If you can take care of a thousand, God will bless you with millions. Real financial healing takes place when you learn how to take care of the little that God has blessed you with already. When you take care of your small apartment, God gives you a mansion or an estate. If you want to truly see blessings in your life, you have to learn to take care of small matters before He can trust you with larger ones.

HAGGAI 1:6-7 reminds us that while we may earn much, it is possible to have very little to show for it.

Ye have sown much, and bring in little; ye eat, but ye have not enough; ye drink, but ye are not filled with drink; ye clothe you, but there is none warm; and he that earneth wages earneth wages to put it into a bag with holes. Thus saith the LORD of hosts; Consider your ways.

We have to understand that it is a true blessing to earn a lot of money, but the reality is that if you spend just as much, the occurrence of one negative financial event can trigger a downward financial spiral. This eventually can have a blow on your relationship and marital pursuits.

9. MAKE WISER FINANCIAL DECISIONS

Seek wisdom in regard to your finances.

James 1:5: If any of you lack wisdom, let him ask of God, that giveth to all men liberally, and upbraideth not; and it shall be given him.

A large number of couples get a feeling of dread when thinking about their finances, and one in twenty people leave bank statements or bills unopened. This can lead to sleepless nights or financial denial, with people refusing to budget, pay bills, or check their bank balance.

Money worries are the leading cause of stress amongst married couples. The impact of this can be detrimental to both physical and mental health.

'We worry because we feel as though life is running away with us and we simply can't keep up. Externalised pressures such as glamorous TV ads and constant advertising can really make people feel inadequate and even further pressured to spend'.

Even more alarming is the link between mental health and financial difficulties.

Many adults with debts have a mental health problem, and one in four people with a mental health problem is also in debt.

'Just as financial difficulties can take their toll on our mental health, mental health problems can also make it harder for us to manage our money, making those financial difficulties more likely, which in turn can make our mental health worse.'

There is also a strong correlation between poor mental health and impulsive and compulsive spending.

UNHELPFUL AND UNHEALTHY THINKING STYLES can also fuel breakdown. Many of our concerns about money are due to the way we think about it and how we construct ideas in our minds.

The first style is BLACK AND WHITE thinking, where a person is unable to see any shades of grey. For example, you are either rich or poor,'

The second unhelpful style is CATASTROPHIC thinking, which starts like a small seed with thoughts like 'I've not got much money this payday'. The person keeps adding to the thought, and it grows larger as they overthink it towards the negative. Eventually, the person is completely wound up and thinks there won't be a roof over their head by the end of the week.

The third style is DISQUALIFYING ANY POSITIVE thoughts and the inability to acknowledge any successes. A person will always be looking to the negative, so even if they have money to pay the bills right now, they will worry about next month.

'There might have been a time when a person still carried the trauma of a past occurrence. They can be triggered right back into that place. Or growing up with parents who worried about making ends meet, and this makes the person anxious, as they have echoes of not having enough.

It is also important to recognise when money worries are being used as a distraction for a different problem. This might be work, a spouse, or an issue around quality of life. So, stop and think about what is really worrying you and be honest with yourself.

If you have unhelpful thinking styles, these can be challenged once you recognise the signals. 'Thoughts are not truths; they are not carved in stone. Once you understand what kind of thinker you are, you can interrupt yourself more effectively. They are just thoughts,'

2 CORINTHIANS 10:5 says, "…Casting down imaginations, and every high thing that exalteth itself against the knowledge of God, and bringing into captivity every thought to the obedience of Christ;"

It is also important to own your financial successes. If money has been tight for one month but you have managed to pay the bills, then be proud of yourself.

The threat of going into arrears can be daunting and produce a range of negative feelings and energy. It can be scary, but the way you respond to these feelings is the most important thing.

Breaking things down into manageable chunks, setting a budget and sticking to it can help you feel more in control. And there are now many online tools and free apps to help you manage your money and keep track of your incomings and outgoings. The Money Advice Service has a range of tools on its website, including a loans calculator, a mortgage affordability calculator, and a budget planner.

Money management apps can also give you live reporting on your spending and send alerts.

Making money is skill but maintaining money is discipline and multiplying money is an art.

If you worry about money to the extent that it is affecting your day-to-day life, especially your marriage or family relationships, then it is important to seek help. There is plenty of advice available from independent organisations like the Money Advice Service, which includes template letters, guides, and budgeting tips.

The Bible says that we are to prosper even as our souls prosper:

Beloved, I wish above all things that thou mayest prosper and be in health, even as thy soul prospereth (3 JOHN 1:2).

Prosperity is more than financial abundance or having a lot of money. You can have money and no prosperity. If your marriage and other relationships are messed up—if your mind, body, or spirit are troubled and you have no peace, then you are not prospering.

Prosperity is a result of salvation. Prosperity is part of our covenant with God and it's the full manifestation of shalom, or peace, which in Hebrew means wholeness, health, healing, favour, and a blessed life, nothing missing, nothing broken. Shalom means you value and enjoy healthy relationships. You enjoy a healthy mind, body, and finances. True prosperity is a result of prospering on the inside.

Being able to love God and love people has everything to do with the position of our hearts. In the New Testament, we've come to see these as abilities that can only come as a result of being filled with the Spirit of God. Empowered by Him, we can be gracious, compassionate, and righteous, which categorically relate to the fruit of the Spirit.

Prosperity is having good relationships, not being a loner and being isolated, not doubting, wavering, or struggling with unbelief, but trusting God and enjoying families and people around you.

You cannot prosper without addressing this area of your life, about the fact that God is your source. The by-product of being fixed and established through the Lord is victory over demons such as foolishness, destruction, procrastination, and confusion. Stability, steadfastness, and single-mindedness are the core and foundation of a prosperous believer's life and a prosperous marriage. Be stabilised and confident, not in yourself but in the Lord. He's got great magnificent plans for you in Christ.

ECCLESIASTES 3:14 KJV – *I know that, whatsoever God doeth, it shall be for ever: nothing can be put to it, nor any thing taken from it: and God doeth it, that men should fear before him.*

Chapter Fourteen

RELATIONSHIP ESSENTIALS

The quality and enduring nature of your relationship with God and people with respect to your spouse and family, will make or break your leadership. It will determine whether you succeed or not.

That axiom is true in every arena of leadership and life, but especially so in the church, business, family and marriage.

When coaching a leader who's in a difficult situation, I ask them a blunt question. "Do they like you?" The response is usually a startled, "What? What do you mean?" "I mean, do the people you work with like you?"

That may seem overly simple for what is likely a complicated situation, but the answer has a significant influence on the outcome.

If the people you work with like you, the potential for resolving conflicts or navigating through difficult circumstances is high. If they don't, you are travelling laboriously uphill, hard and difficult struggle for sure.

An important question is, how much do you invest in relationships? It's like putting money in the bank. The more you have invested, the greater the returns, and over time, it's compounding in your favour.

In contrast, if you make more withdrawals than contributions relationally, over time, the people you work with won't want to work with you. They won't have regards for you as a user and taker.

It's easy to think you don't always have enough time to invest in relationships, but it never takes long to be kind, and that's a good start.

Whether you are naturally good with people or need to work at it, it's often the absence of basics that takes a leader out. When you're on the run and under pressure, it's easy to cut corners and skip over the oil that keeps relationships running smoothly.

Here is some really good news: those relational basics take very little time.

THE ESSENTIALS

1. TREAT PEOPLE, ESPECIALLY YOUR SPOUSE WITH RESPECT

To communicate and demonstrate value to another human being is a great honour paid to them.

It's a truly moving moment for them that will be remembered for a long time. And while one day they may have forgotten the specifics, they'll never forget how you made them feel.

When it's tough to see the value in someone, look at them as you imagine Jesus would. Their value will jump out at you.

2. EXPRESS APPRECIATION

It takes a couple of seconds to say thank you and less than a minute to express sincere appreciation.

I'm not suggesting it's a race to see how fast you can say thank you, but merely that you have time. If we don't express appreciation enough, it's because we were too focused on the task and not enough on the people involved in our lives with me on it.

3. ENCOURAGE YOUR SPOUSE OFTEN AND GENEROUSLY

You can't encourage people too much; you just can't. Encouragement is an act of cheering one another up and on, saying you're highly honoured and affectionately appreciated

If you're like me, you might say you don't need a tonne of appreciation or encouragement, but let's be honest, doesn't it feel good when it comes your way?

The truth is, we all need it, and it's equally important that we give it often. The single most important factor in encouraging someone is to make it sincere.

4. GIVE THEM BENEFIT OF THE DOUBT

Giving the benefit of the doubt is needed the most with the people you are closest to like your spouse and those you work with the most.

If someone said something that really bugged you, or you received an email that caught you off guard, or someone made a decision you disagree with, extend grace. Don't let it fester; assume the best and talk with them. It's almost always better than it appears.

5. LOOK FOR THE BEST IN YOUR SPOUSE.

If you look for the best in every person, you will find it. You will be glad you did as it stands to benefit you so much.

There is something special within every person, and as a spiritual leader, it's part of your responsibility to help them discover and utilise it for the greater good of others.

It's true that some people can make this challenging, but you can make it productive. And if they genuinely are difficult, extend grace.

A good starting place with a difficult person or spouse is to learn a little about their story. That often helps adjust your perspective and gives you insight.

Therefore, look for the best in people, you will always find it.

6. PRACTISE KINDNESS NATURALLY

Kindness is a commonly overlooked yet essential aspect of relationships building. Be kindly affectionate to one another. You have to be kind in your conversations.

We tend to focus more on aspects such as tough-minded decision-making, strategy, and bold vision. That's good and necessary, but kindness is an essential human quality that allows trust, connection, and genuine exchange to take place.

Wise people recognise that kindness brings peace and joy into even the most pressure-filled situations.

Kindness embraces three crucial elements: genuine humility, a desire to serve others, and personal contentment. Joy at last.

7. LISTEN WELL

Be quick to hear and slow to speak. Listen, listen, listen. This is a skill. Listening 101 if you put it that way because it's so essential.

There are a few aspects of human interaction that prioritise esteem for others more than listening.

Listening communicates value, respect, and love. The speed of culture, social media, and a general lack of connection have hurt the ability and even the desire to fully listen at a heart level. If you fall into that trap, it will hurt your marriage.

Listening at a heart level means focusing entirely on the person with good intent, and your responses should reflect that you understand.

Prioritise listening for others more than just talking.

8. LIVE WITH A GENEROUS SPIRIT

Couples who possess a generous spirit tend to build successful and exceptional marriages than those who do not. There is something compelling and inviting about the disposition to give rather than hold back.

Generosity is often financial, kindness of heart, bearing gifts but there is so much more to it, such as giving your time, offering words of affirmation, sharing ideas, helping to solve a problem, and demonstrating love.

9. OWN YOUR MISTAKES

People do not respect and eventually stop following personalities who don't own and take responsibility for their mistakes. There's an emotional and mental disconnection and a subtle silent unfollow.

We all experience failures, setbacks, mistakes, and decisions that didn't turn out well.

If you make a mess, clean it up. Don't back the bus up over someone else; just own the situation, learn from it, and move forward. Your wife, your husband and your children will trust and respect you for it.

10. GENUINELY CARE ABOUT PEOPLE

People don't care how much you know till they know how much you care.

There are very few personalities who don't care about people, but it's easy to forget to show that you care when you're under pressure and have so much to do and accomplish.

You can't learn to care, but you can ask God to help you care. Through prayer, God can increase your empathy, compassion, and general desire for others to thrive.

Care is rarely felt at high speed; you have to slow down to find someone's heartfelt need.

9 781739 214623